Praise for *Letters from the Closet*

"Rarely do I get excited about a book that comes my way, but *Letters from the Closet* is beautifully written, intelligent, multi-layered, sensitive, and alarmingly mature. I promise you, you will enjoy this book for its art and its insight. As I read it, I felt that my heart was more active than my mind, but both were at full speed. You need to read it more than once, because there's a lot going on. If you don't read it at least once, you're missing out on a rare treat. There is not a word out of place in this skillfully written book."

—Thomas Moore, *New York Times* bestselling author
of *Care of the Soul*

"*Letters from the Closet* is a beautiful book: an unusually honest memoir that explores the need for self-discovery and exposes the dangers of self-delusion."

—Scott Jordan Harris, UK correspondent for Roger Ebert
and culture blogger for *The Daily Telegraph*

"I felt deep stirrings in the first few pages of this remarkable book, stirrings that I eventually came to recognize as healing—my own. With her exquisite prose, wisdom, wit, and most of all courage, Amy Hollingsworth shows what wondrous things can happen when we open our respective closets and let the darkness meet the light. After the privilege of reading her here, I know I feel less alone."

—Tim Madigan, award-winning newspaper journalist and
author of *I'm Proud of You: My Friendship with Fred Rogers*

"The relationships that wield the most influence in our lives are often complex. They defy tidy categories, intermingle joy with pain, teach us how to live, and surpass even the power of death. *Letters from the Closet* poignantly captures just such a relationship. Part memoir, part love letter, and part tribute, the book shows how words, letters, books, and dreams are woven together to shape a life, a soul, and a love."

—Karen Swallow Prior,
author of *Booked: Literature in the Soul of Me*

"In this unique memoir, Amy Hollingsworth opens the door to her intimate correspondence with her extraordinary high school English teacher. I had anticipated that *Letters from the Closet* was going to be about a teacher's struggle with sexual orientation, but the book turned out to be even more about the author's own self-exploration and discovery. By sharing the healing power of their mutual self-disclosure, Amy invites us to join them in lifting off our own masks—and identifying our own gifts and life purpose."

—Dr. David G. Myers, social psychologist, author,
and professor of psychology at Hope College

"Psychologically astute and literarily informed, Amy Hollingsworth makes poetry of closets—closed ones, bursting ones, neat ones, and fearful ones. Yet there is one closet she does not mention, and it is that one that is central to this deeply insightful memoir. It is the one that a child enters, one filled with ghosts and frightful encounters, and one through which she can only feel her way until she bursts through the back and falls into maturity, wisdom, and what might well be called New Creation."

—Jim Street, pastor, North River Church, Lawrenceville, GA

Letters from
the Closet

Ten Years of Correspondence That Changed My Life

AMY HOLLINGSWORTH

HOWARD BOOKS
A Division of Simon & Schuster, Inc.

New York   Nashville   London   Toronto   Sydney   New Delhi

Howard Books
A Division of Simon & Schuster, Inc.
1230 Avenue of the Americas
New York, NY 10020

First Howard Books hardcover edition May 2013

HOWARD and colophon are trademarks of Simon & Schuster, Inc.

For information about special discounts for bulk purchases,
please contact Simon & Schuster Special Sales at 1-866-506-1949
or business@simonandschuster.com.

The Simon & Schuster Speakers Bureau can bring authors to your live event. For more information or to book an event, contact the Simon & Schuster Speakers Bureau at 1-866-248-3049 or visit our website at www.simonspeakers.com.

Designed by Davina Mock-Maniscalco

Manufactured in the United States of America

10   9   8   7   6   5   4   3   2   1

Library of Congress Cataloging-in-Publication Data

Hollingsworth, Amy.
   Letters from the closet : ten years of correspondence that changed my life /
Amy Hollingsworth.—1st Howard Books hardcover ed.
      p. cm.
   1. Hollingsworth, Amy. 2. Hollingsworth, Amy—Relations with gay men.
3. Hollingsworth, Amy—Correspondence. 4. Authors, American—21st
century—Biography. 5. Gay men—Relations with heterosexual women—
Biography. 6. Teacher-student relationships—Biography. I. Title.
   PS3608.O48485Z46 2013
   816'.6—dc23
   [B]

                                                   2012034297

ISBN 978-1-4516-6677-9
ISBN 978-1-4516-6678-6 (ebook)

For John.
Enjoy.

CONTENTS

1

INTRODUCTION

Boy Meets Girl

I destroyed every page of my college journals. There were eight journals in all, two for each year, every empty space within swallowed up by my perfect Catholic school script: a chronicle of my life as a coed. I wasn't getting rid of evidence exactly (although there was much to incriminate me), but I was starting over, and this was proof I wasn't that person anymore. I can't remember if I burned all the pages or simply tore them to shreds to prevent their being pieced back together (should the garbageman be tempted) and threw them away. In either case, they were disposed of.

I have a friend whose husband demanded she destroy a photo of Elvis kissing her during one of his Vegas performances, taken before she'd even met her husband. He wanted proof she wasn't that person anymore. She promised she would, then mailed it off to a friend for safekeeping. I wish I had done the same with my journals, but I was young and convinced that rashness was the quickest path to righteousness.

It was an act of obedience in my mind, a declaration of allegiance, like Abraham laying Isaac on the altar. Except no one had bothered to stop my sacrifice. No substitution was made for my lost darlings, those early glimpses into college life: how I felt reading Milton at the picnic table outside my dorm, what it was like to pore over Freud in the undergrad library. Lost, too, were accounts of the long-distance phone conversations between me and my high school English teacher, who was lamenting my absence as newspaper editor.

My high school English teacher was young and alive, so he lacked the gravitas that comes with being old and dead.

My high school English teacher was of course young and alive, so he lacked the gravitas that comes with being old and dead; but his impact was equally noted alongside Milton's and Freud's, scratched into the pages of my journals. Not a word of our phone conversations survived, although his many letters did. I don't know why those didn't get expunged or extinguished along with the rest; some were more inappropriate than my college misdeeds. Still, they had been preserved through moves from dorm room to apartment, during the transition from college to grad school, kept safe during trips overseas, when all my worldly possessions were either locked away in my parents' basement or stored in a friend's garage. Childhood photos had been destroyed when the basement flooded but his letters escaped both water and fire (if it turns out I did burn the journals). Ten years after the first letter was sent, they found a permanent home in my closet.

Sometimes he would write as if he were a character from a book or a play I was assigned to read; other times he would include snippets from the novel he was writing. (He often complained that writing to me cut into his novel-writing time.) His long letters shifted between tender affection and brutal honesty, and in one full of the latter he called me emotionally shallow for participating in the bacchanalia of college life (his vices were more sophisticated). Worse, he said that though he had carefully nurtured my writing throughout high school, he didn't see me writing the great American novel. "You don't have the patience for it," he wrote.

I was eighteen; he was thirty.

I was playing at life, he was living it, squeezing out what he could, sometimes enduring it. He had always known he would die young, most likely by his own hand, but in the end his death was out of his control. "I will shout 'yippee!' on my deathbed," he insisted years before, but I don't think he did, because the choice had been taken from him. His brooding poet wasn't for show. There was a reason for his unhappiness.

Would I mourn him? He wasn't near death when he

asked, just curious. The question came in the form of a hypo-thetical ("if I were pushed off a cliff") in one of his early let-ters. He guessed I wouldn't, because of my emotional shallowness. He was wrong. I do mourn him. He was wrong about something else. I do have the patience.

Not only because I waited for our story to end before committing it to paper, but because I've lived long enough to figure out that no part of my life should be ripped to shreds or set on fire. Or hidden away in a closet.

What Connected Us

It was not love at first sight.

We met when I was fifteen, my first year in a public high school, where I struggled to find my sense of being and style after having been cloistered and uniformed most of my life. I didn't make wise choices in that brave new world: I couldn't yet help the thick lenses poking through the wire rims of my glasses, but it was free will that prompted the canary yellow jumper and the mass of natural curls cut into a perfectly symmetrical circle atop my head. That's what he noticed, those were his first words to me, that I reminded him of an iridescent Jesus in *Godspell*. Contact lenses, blow dryers, and less festive clothing eventually cured my ills; and a few years later he would say my prettiness had made me callous.

He was tall, sandy blond, wore pointy-toed boots. He

struggled with style, too, though intentionally, refusing to cede the middle part in his hair, hanging on to his hip-waisted corduroys as an act of protest (when no one protested anymore). A child of the sixties stuck in the sixties, living in the seventies. Meet Jesus from *Godspell.*

There was more, of course, to our relationship in those early days, more to our commiseration (we were both keeping secrets), more to our chemistry (we both wanted to know what it was like to be in love). We dreamed of becoming writers, talked about writing books together. I had been the poet-in-residence at my little parochial school; he put in his eight hours of teaching each day for a coveted few at the typewriter at night, tapping out the great American novel.

That was it, really: what connected us, from the very beginning, were words. I'd known I wanted to be a writer since second grade, since a very specific afternoon in second grade. My teacher then was a woman, young, pretty, and childless. The school couldn't afford individual textbooks, so the whole of our education was dispensed by oral tradition (that is, Mrs. Hill read to us from the sole textbook she held in her hands). There was something soothing and womblike about those hot afternoons (no money for air-conditioning, either), when Mrs. Hill would turn off the fluorescent lights above, direct us to lay our heads on our desks, and read to us. It was fortuitous that my ears and not my eyes were the main vehicles of learning back

> *What connected us, from the very beginning, were words.*
>
>

then, especially when it came time for our first poetry lesson. I don't even remember what poem she read to us in that darkened classroom, only that the words were altogether different from those that taught us about dinosaurs or subtraction or catechism. I raised my head from my desk to better catch the words as they dipped and rose, hesitated with Mrs. Hill's breath, and then began to rise and fall again. I knew nothing about rhythm, meter, or flow, only that these words traveled in waves, making their way around the classroom like a troubadour whose instrument played loudest at my desk.

I couldn't wait to get off the bus that afternoon so that I could start writing. Nothing else mattered but getting alone with pencil and paper. It didn't have to make sense as long as it rhymed, so my first attempts at poetry were hideous concoctions, like Frankenstein's monster with badly matched limbs.

The muse must favor that age with both desire and misdirection. The unnamed narrator in *Zorba the Greek* relates a similar experience from his own childhood, when he reads a book in school about a boy who falls into a well, only to discover a magical world below. The story itself was not meant to be instructive or inspiring; it was simply a vehicle to teach him the second half of the alphabet. But as he spelled out each word, he longed to follow in the footsteps of the boy in the story, to enter the same magic city. The words, like the troubadour at my desk, caught hold of him, transported him, prompted him to action.

I created Frankenstein monsters; he went home and poised himself at the family well. He was sure he could make out the edges of the honey-filled lake described in the story, and his body reached toward it. An ever-seeing mother caught him by the belt at the moment of descent, sparing or denying him.

Perhaps I felt the tug of some external restraint—not as a child, but later in high school, after we first met—pulling me away from the story, from the world my teacher would create for us to live in. It doesn't matter now that the wellspring is gone. I can only gather up his words like rainwater in a cistern and fall in.

> *I can only gather up his words like rainwater in a cistern and fall in.*

An Unlikely Prophet

After our first semester together, my teacher handed me the following note, which I saved in a scrapbook of my high school years. I didn't destroy my high school scrapbook as I did my college journals, because the scrapbook was propaganda. It included only the good press, excising the shameful and the uncomfortable: photo evidence that I had once been fat; mention of my dad's confession that he was an alcoholic—on New Year's Eve of all times; and my parents' subsequent separation (Mom moved out once her spouse came to). Instead there were photos of me as the graduating class's malnourished valedictorian, an original handwritten copy of my commencement speech, and the newspaper clipping in which I was named "Most Likely to Succeed." (Because I was the newspaper's editor, reporters from the junior class had to put the issue together, in order not to ruin the surprise. They did a terrible job.)

Even as I built the monument there was evidence of a crack, a leak in my PR. It was my teacher's note—the title of the book, he said, that most reminded him of me after our first semester together—and it linked me to fools, fools seeking an illusory salvation, fools on a voyage to eternity. "Amy has set sail on a ship of fools" is how I read it. Yesterday I discovered that Katherine Anne Porter's *Ship of Fools* (my teacher misspelled her first name) was the number-one book on the *New York Times* bestseller list the day I was born. What are the chances? What are the odds he would pick a book so significantly tied to my birth a decade and a half before? That's the way things went on from there. He was irreligious, antireligious; but in ways neither of us could understand, he connected things in my life. Past things to present things, present things to future things. An unlikely prophet who saw into my future, the seer who saw through me. It was his job to remind me I wasn't what I seemed.

For AMY

Ship of Fools

Kathryn Anne Porter

2

SKELETONS IN THE CLOSET

Secrets That Dance

If you can't get rid of the skeleton in your closet,
you'd best teach it to dance.
—GEORGE BERNARD SHAW

I fainted in the hallway.

That was the story, what he wrote in his note to Mrs. B., another English teacher. I fainted in the hallway en route to her class, just outside his door, and that's why I was late. Not that we had been alone in his empty classroom and couldn't be bothered by the bell sounding for classes to change, for the halls to fill.

Mrs. B. believed in second chances, had divorced and remarried the same man. She would have forgiven me if she had known our secret. But she never found out. She kept a concerned eye on me during class and afterward asked him about it in the teachers' lounge. Yes, I had fallen dead away, just like that, right in front of his door.

Later Mrs. B. heard the rumor that John and I (my teacher's name was John) were secretly engaged to be married. She asked him about it, again in the teachers' lounge. It was no rumor, he assured her, and she believed him, just like with the fainting.

Love is an imprecise science; there's no clear way of predicting who will attach to whom or for what reasons. (Or in Mrs. B.'s case, how many times.) Maybe love is more alchemy than science, an attempt to transmute the baser things in life into something lofty. And then if you want to avoid love, you do it backward. You turn the gold into something worthless instead of the other way around. It's a distraction tactic, like teaching the skeleton in your closet to dance. Then no one knows the truth about you.

When I was in eighth grade, my teacher Mr. K. rode his bike to my house after school. Mr. K. was in his twenties and single, and he would stand at the door as his classroom emptied, and he'd catch my eye as I exited the classroom across the hall and wink at me so that only I could see. I called him a sadist once for banning our dance team from an afternoon assembly for some small infraction. It had been one of our vocabulary words that week, and I thought he would be impressed by my speedy application of it. Instead he made me kneel on chalk in the hallway and balance dictionaries in upturned hands. (The punishment called for Bibles but there weren't any around, even in a Catholic school.) The chalk dug into my bare knees; my uniform skirt, while the pre-scribed length—it had to touch the floor when kneeling in veneration—wasn't long enough to fold under. There was no prescription for kneeling in punishment. The whole scene meant, I think, that if I had misapplied the word originally, I was proven right a few minutes later. He was probably agitated by the fact that I told my parents he stopped by the house when they weren't home, and when the nuns found out they banned any interaction outside the classroom. Dented knees from the sadist, my punishment for not keeping a secret.

That's what happens when your breast buds sprout in fourth grade. The summer after Mr. K. cycled to my house, a middle-aged, married lifeguard at our swim club—also a teacher—invited me to sit on his lap when no one was looking. This time I didn't tell anyone. If it's true that Amazon warriors cut off their right breasts for better aim with a bow, my battle plan was less drastic but equally effective. I discovered that if you don't eat, what makes you feminine goes away. It's deflation as opposed to mutilation. It's much harder to be desired by men when you're shaped like a twelve-year-old boy. Being flat-chested and slim-hipped was my armor, and starving myself assured I was always wearing it. I was not the sole warrior. Poet Louise Glück writes poignantly of coming of age and discovering her own growing breasts, her "interfering flesh" that she

I discovered that if you don't eat, what makes you feminine goes away.

would sacrifice by starvation "until the limbs were free of blossom." That's what I wanted, too, to be free of blossom.

That of course caused problems when I occasionally ate like a normal person and the weight came back, refilling the feminine spaces. One afternoon my government teacher, standing in the back of the classroom, had students march one by one to the front of the class, sit on a stool, and answer questions from the chapter we had been assigned. Several students had come and gone unsuccessfully and then when he called my name, I assumed it was because he was certain I'd know the answers. I walked from the back row to the front of the class, sat on the stool, waited for the question. No question came. "Thanks so much for that, Amy," he said. "You can go back to your seat now." There was tittering, and a clap or two, as I resumed the catwalk back to my desk. Flesh was interfering. I skipped lunch that day.

The skeleton in my closet was a literal one; it was me, on my way to becoming one. It was an easy enough secret to hide in a large family, when siblings had greater problems than mine. When parents had greater problems than mine. Easy enough to say I had a big lunch at school or an early dinner so that I could concentrate on schoolwork. To hide the laxatives, to lock my bedroom door when I slept in a trash bag (an old wrestler's trick to sweat off a few pounds overnight), to gather up the loose hair from the shower drain. Easy enough to say my period stopped because I was exercising more, although that was mostly true. Then the return to food, after weeks of abstinence (the first time I ate during one November was Thanksgiving Day), meant quick weight gain as my body hoarded what little it could. My secret, then, was partially hidden by the seesaw of loss and gain. You're fine, my mother said. You're the one kid we never worry about, my father said. The diagnosis is malnutrition, the doctor said.

No one raised an eyebrow, because it was impossible to believe that a straight-A student from the suburbs, who governed her class and edited her school newspaper while holding down a part-time job, could suffer the same fate as a war-torn Biafran child. So my skeleton kept dancing.

Uncomfortably Close

I have dreams about John all the time; they started just after he died. There is a common thread that runs through them all: we are looking for an empty room, a quiet place to reconnect. We are rarely successful, though. The timing is always off.

In one dream we are at a school event, a reunion, and there are so many people in attendance that we are shoved into the corner of a classroom. (In real life there was always an empty classroom where we could ignore the bell, ignore the world, and excuse our behavior with a tardy slip.) A female teacher is looking on, watching us closely. She never takes her eyes off us. I lift my arms over my head and clasp my hands together and slowly lower them around John's neck. It's not a show of affection; it's a space saver as we are pushed closer and closer together by the crowd, pressed into each other. I look him in the eyes and quietly ask, "Are you still tormented?"

I look him in the eyes and quietly ask, "Are you still tormented?"

He is surprised. He laughs but there's sadness in it. Yes, he says.

A Third Secret

There was not much known about anorexia nervosa when I was in high school, and the phrase for John's secret (or the divulging of his secret) hadn't even been coined yet. I guess John's skeleton was himself, too, not starving, but hiding. The phrase *to come out of the closet* actually sprang from the imagery of a skeleton in the closet and was first used of alcoholics in the fifties who confessed their dependence and sobered up. That means my dad was the first among us to come staggering out of the closet, a bourbon-soaked skeleton, when he declared his alcoholism on New Year's Eve. The admission of his secret during my high school years pushed my secret further into the closet. The universe tends to even itself out, I guess; when one secret is exposed, another becomes more deeply entrenched. It's more likely I saw the consequences of his unveiled secret and graciously declined. Hiding created less of a stir, led to less drastic changes. Our family could handle only one problem at a time and only if forced to. We had limited resources. Once I ran away from home and no one noticed, so I walked home in the dark and hid in the garage until someone found me. It became a family joke: remember when Amy ran away to the garage? No one ever asked why I had run away. When no one asks, then no one knows the truth about you.

Even John and I didn't know the particulars of each other's secrets, not at first. Those confessions came later, through the letters, when geographic distance granted us immunity. What we did know is that the other was playacting. That neither of us was who we appeared to be. When we conspired to create a third secret, we had no idea we were protecting the other; we intended only to protect ourselves. We invented a love affair. John spread the rumor about the secret engagement, but by then there were already suspicions because of all the time we spent together. Maybe that's why Mrs. B. believed him. This third secret served a twofold purpose: it protected John from rumors that he was gay (he was old enough and attractive enough to be married, after all), and it provided a barrier between me and the other male faculty. Banished were the winking sadists, swimsuit-clad pedophiles, rear-viewing government teachers. Our mutual secret hid our individual secrets— that we were both disguising our sexuality—even if we didn't know it at the time.

We must have been pretty convincing. When John picked me up one evening in his pale blue Barracuda to attend an awards dinner for my winning a statewide essay contest, attendees from other high schools mistook us for a married couple. We could have taken our act on the road. I guess in some ways we were using each other, turning gold into something worthless. We conspired as reverse alchemists. But love is tricky. It can take something as flimsy as a lie and bind two people together with it, pressing them into a corner until the truth will out.

In some ways we were using each other, turning gold into something worthless.

The Letters

My first semester in college was coming to a close, and already I had received a dozen letters from John. My new Southern friends had adjusted to my oddities as a misplaced Midwesterner, but this relationship was something they couldn't understand. Why the late-night phone calls from a high school English teacher? Why the long letters? If it was a charade for high school, as I conceded, why continue it now?

> You know, when we see each other when you come home, it could be awkward,

he had written in his precise tiny script.

After writing such letters, you might feel funny seeing me. I think we ought to plan out some sort of scene we can stage when we first see each other again. Maybe you could appear at my classroom door sort of silently all of the sudden and then I could look up and just sort of silently mouth "Amy." Then we could stare passionately at each other for a couple of beats. Then I'd rise and you'd step into the room all the way. There would be a hush from my students as they'd realize they were witnessing history. Someone would surely take pictures.

Here he made up a mock headline for the school newspaper we had worked on together: "Teacher Meets Student After Weeks of Separation."

Then I'd sort of chuckle in a low, deep, very masculine voice and you'd throw back your hair and smile. I'd finally

*say aloud, "Amy," and you'd laugh, lightly.
Then we'd race for each other and meet
in a passionate embrace and declare
our eternal love for each other.*

I read this letter, and it reminds me of my dream. More a parody of my dream. In both the dream and the letter, John and I are being reunited. In both the dream and the letter, the reunion takes place in a crowded classroom. But there is one big difference: in the scene he stages we are still pretending. Our skeletons are two-stepping for show. There's no real honesty, no real closeness, no sad laugh admitting torment.

Of course his letters became more serious, less silly as time went on. Later he would even write: "A teacher is like a book, wasted until he's read. The student has to do that. You've done that." But I think he was being hopeful because I hadn't done it yet. Not really.

"A teacher is like a book, wasted until he's read. The student has to do that."

One day I would. But it would require a quiet place to reconnect. The stage would have to empty of other characters; the playacting would have to be over for good. That's what we both wanted. To be read. To be asked. To have someone in our lives we couldn't fool.

3

FIBBER MCGEE'S CLOSET

Stuff Comes Tumbling Out

I think I've reached a point where I realize
that what's most important is peace—not happiness,
not fame, not popularity, not sex, not money, not ego,
not having a good time, not even helping the world.
No, it's peace that I've come to see as important.
There is much to be said for harmony. I think I know
now why Emily Dickinson never left her room—
there was nothing out there she needed.

—JOHN

There are different kinds of closets. Not all of them hide skeletons. Some of them preserve relics. A famous theater teacher said that the gift of being a writer is being able to turn the cleaning of a closet into an inventory of love and loss. That's what really started it all. I was cleaning out my closet and found his letters. The relics of our relationship. Our inventory of love and loss.

I've tried to tell our story before now. The timing was always off. I told John in a dream that I wanted to write about our relationship, and he didn't object, just offered this: it's still liquid, you know. I think he meant the relationship was still in motion, the conclusion not yet set. I would learn things as I went along. I wonder if he thought I wasn't ready. In the dream he said he was going ahead of me, moving to a new city. He would call for me, I would join him, the following year. He planned to buy a house with a writing room. That's what closets were originally used for. They weren't for clothing or storage or even hiding skeletons, but private rooms built for prayer or study or writing. But *private* doesn't mean alone. The oldest usage includes the idea of having a close encounter with someone. Two people in intimate private conversation are said to be "closeted." It's a quiet place to reconnect.

It's funny because when I left high school, John and I promised each other that if neither of us got married (and neither of us planned to), we would buy a house and write books together. Now he had bought a house. Soon we'd be writing a book together.

A year has passed since the dream, and just as he foretold, I now have the time and space and opportunity to tell our story. I even have my own writing room, the quiet place that eluded us for years. We are back in our empty classroom.

One of the things we have in common, he wrote in a letter, is that we are always trying to get things to fall into place. And we are both able to get things to fall into place by the same means: we write about them. That's the only way you arrive at a sense of peace about things, he said, by sorting through them, by getting them to fall into place. By putting them on paper. That's how I would make peace with his death, with how our relationship ended. But I needed a guiding image, some kind of theme or concept, to help me sort through the different aspects of our relationship.

The closet imagery fits us. His letters had been written from the confines and protection of the closet he was still hiding in; letters that were read, cherished, and then locked away for decades in my closet.

Letters from the closet—written from his, rescued from mine.

Now there is a third closet, my writing room, where sorting through the letters, getting them to fall into place, would bring us peace. Then there would be nothing out there we needed.

Letters from the closet— written from his, rescued from mine.

Locked Away

I think John would have liked the idea that I locked away his letters in my closet, as if they were state secrets. "I have lock'd the letter in my closet," says a character in *King Lear,* to shield the wrong eyes from its dangerous content. Some of John's letters were dangerous, too. Some are still difficult to read. But those letters came later. The early letters were silly and melodramatic. He created mischief at home, too, by finding little ways to keep the rumors circulating at my high school. When the new style sheet for the school newspaper was distributed in the fall, every single citation example contained my name; the only other name mentioned was his. There were more proclamations of undying love, threats of suicide if I didn't return home, and worse, a marriage proposal.

OK, I understand what I have to do now; I realize what the final course of action is. I didn't want to do this—I want you to know this. I was hoping we could get around such a drastic action. But, I can see no possible alternative now. The die is cast; the stone is set. I offered you your editorship again; you turned it down. I offered you free rein to do what you wanted on the paper; you turned it down. I offered you my position-advisor; you turned it down. So now it's the final sacrifice. Come back-you can marry me. No, no-off your knees; say no more. Tears aren't necessary. I understand; I understand.

There were attempts to make each other jealous; I tried to find his replacement in a college professor, and he pretended to have found the new me back at my high school:

Are you trying to make me jealous? You know I worshipped you for your mind and not your body.

And then a reversal on that stand:

She [he was referring to another student or maybe it was Mrs. B.] *honestly believes that I love you and would jump into bed with you if you'd give the word. Well, I don't love you, anyway.*

At some point we moved past the charade. We took a step forward, supposing we were making progress because we were no longer pretending. We turned down a well-worn path, mimicking the great teacher–student relationships we had read about in books. The fictional roles appealed to us; we both processed life through literature. It also dragged us away from the flames for a while, the reverse alchemy having backfired on us. It was a rich, exciting time, the relationship every student longs for, the life lesson stuff that Mitch Albom gleans from his dying professor in *Tuesdays with Morrie*. We could be *Tuesdays with Morrie*, I've often thought, if Morrie were young and gay and Mitch Albom were a woman.

> *We could be Tuesdays with Morrie, I've often thought, if Morrie were young and gay and Mitch Albom were a woman.*

We didn't plan to write letters after high school. When he handed me a homemade graduation gift, he thought it would be our last exchange. It was a book of quotes he had handpicked for me. He had typed up the quotes on his old typewriter, the same one he was using to write the great American novel. The typos had been corrected by hand. The quotes were divided into categories (he wanted them to fall into place): on writing, on security, on existence. He had cut out pictures from magazines to illustrate each category, glued them to typing paper, and stapled the whole thing together. On the front cover, under another pasted photograph, he had written that since he would no longer be around to goad me into greatness, these inspiring quotes would have to do. He was my supernatural mentor, my protective guardian, bestowing the amulet—these most carefully chosen words—that would guide me on my journey when he was no longer there. It was a symbolic gesture, a way to ensure peace in the trials ahead. Neither of us knew at the time that he would continue to "goad me into greatness" with his long letters. The words I needed were not Oscar Wilde's or J. D. Salinger's or Anne Morrow Lindbergh's but his.

The Doctor Is In

When I taught psychology at the university, I asked another professor if there were any Freudians in the psychology department. There was only one Freudian on campus, he said, and he was in the English department.

John was surprised when I went to graduate school to study psychology. For one, he thought I would make a lousy shrink ("I still see you as a lawyer. You're too self-centered to be a shrink"). But he shouldn't have been surprised because he, as my unlikely prophet, predicted it during my senior year of high school. It was my last semester with him, and he did not hand out book titles as he did my freshman year. He gave each student in his Honors class a quote that he felt best described him or her. He had given me two quotes (after all, we were engaged), the first of which was an excerpt from Patrick

Dennis's book *3D*: "If God in Heaven failed, there was always God in Vienna. As a team, God and Freud were unbeatable."

I knew nothing of Freud at the time and had little interest in what he had to say, or in what God had to say for that matter, despite my parochial school upbringing. I thought John had misfired, even though his ascribing *Ship of Fools* to me had been painfully accurate a few years before, and he didn't even know me well then. But just a few months into my first year of college, I dismayed my English professors when I bounded into the registrar's office to declare a double major, adding psychology to my degree program.

The culprit was my introduction to the psyche in my Psych 101 class. My attraction to this concept and its architect was neither intriguing nor multilayered; I think Freud himself would be hard-pressed to recover a sexual subtext. It's just that Freud looked below the surface of things, to the unconscious, which was an epiphany to someone who had been raised on the rim. Digging below the surface allowed me to open up, and John was quick to fill the empty space— with the grit and gore of his own unconscious stirrings. There is always a place for a Freudian in the English department.

For a while, I really did think Freud was God in Vienna. Exploring the psyche—and the idea that there were things at work influencing my behavior that I was completely unaware of—was akin to discovering a magic city, like the one in the well the narrator in *Zorba the Greek* longs to fall into. (Of course he nearly killed himself taking the plunge.) It was a time of wide-eyed wonder, and John joined in, fueled it, saw it as his chance to become the Plato to my Aristotle (or Freud to my Jung). This was a new direction in our relationship, and it was Sigmund who had opened the door.

The door, unfortunately, had been closed for a reason. Opening it meant releasing the crammed-up emotions that had been stuffed inside. That's why I call this stage in our relationship Fibber McGee's closet. Fibber McGee's closet was a running gag on the famous radio show *Fibber McGee and Molly,* and it was such a popular gimmick it became a catchphrase for a closet so jam-packed that its contents fall on your head when you open the door. It was a sound gag that spilled over in television with visual depictions of the exploding closet seen on everything from *Looney Tunes* to *The Dick Van Dyke Show* to *Star Trek,* where Captain Kirk opens a cargo bay and is covered by a cascade of purring tribbles.

It was a daunting task to approach that door, one that John was willing to help with but not quite ready to undertake himself. "That may be one reason why I could never buy the idea of a god—how horrible for anyone to see into my soul," he wrote in a letter. But then if you pack lots of stuff away in your closet and rarely visit it, if you lock it up and don't deal with what's in there, you never quite work things out. Things don't fall into place until they first fall out.

Things don't fall into place until they first fall out.

Alone in the Library

Your letter made me laugh again when I pictured you, on your own, sitting in the library and reading Freud. Surely you remember Danny Saunders from The Chosen *who did the exact same thing. I can just see you with earlocks and bad eyes!*

I didn't have earlocks or bad eyes, but I did sit in the library alone reading Freud, like Danny Saunders, the Jewish schoolboy in Chaim Potok's novel *The Chosen*. We had read the novel in John's class; it amused him to think I was acting out a scene from one of his favorite books. Danny Saunders had a secret—just like John, just like me. Danny's secret was reading Freud, who would have been denounced in his strict religious home. Danny's other secret was that he didn't want to become a rabbi like his father; he wanted to study psychology. He wanted to explore the psyche. Of course he couldn't communicate his desires to his father, who never spoke to Danny except to discuss religious tradition. Danny was raised in silence. His defiance in the library was the first step in breaking free from his family.

Perhaps we did have something more in common, Danny and I, sitting alone in the library reading Freud, digging deeper. We were both learning that it's impossible to understand the psyche apart from the psychosis of your own family. It was the hours alone in the library that first made me think I may have been pointing my bony finger in the wrong direction. Maybe, just maybe, my secret—the years of starving myself—had less to do with shielding my breast buds from leering teachers and more to do with a family who doesn't ask why a child runs away.

Secret Society

I'm always amazed that anorexics tend to follow the same patterns of behavior; it's as if they've all been assigned the same manual, or initiated into a secret society, completely unaware there are other members. While the physical symptoms are remarkably similar, an early study on anorexics found only one psychological characteristic in common: an intellectual aloofness from their environment. I had been detached. Not eating helped to keep me detached. It eliminated conversation around the dinner table, cut down on family interaction. A secret by nature isolates its keeper, which isn't always a bad thing depending on the available company. It wraps you in a protective bubble.

You know, after your phone call the other night, I started worrying that maybe you weren't really as happy as you sound. It was just something in your tone when you said goodbye. I don't know. Then it hit me that after all our "up" letters, we'd never want to admit a down time to each other. And finally, I'd heard some rumors about your parents having some marital problems and true or not, I thought that might be bothering you. But again, I figure that you're capable of dealing with things and I hope you realize you can always write about or talk about the down things, too. Still, it makes me feel better to have said all that.

Yes, there was that. The marital problems were not new; they began while I was still in high school. My mother had moved into her own apartment after my dad went to rehab, stopped drinking, started attending smoke-filled AA meetings. (Freud would say the AA-ers traded one oral fixation, drinking, for another, smoking. That might explain the free-flowing coffee, too.)

It was a trial separation, they said. On the day my mom moved out, I pretended to be sick so I wouldn't have to help her load up the U-Haul, so as not to be an accessory to her crime. I stayed in bed and wrote out my applications for college scholarships. I was detached, aloof. And hungry. (I had an anti-oral fixation.) Thankfully, the hunger pangs stopped trying after a while; they gave up, frustrated by their inability to get my attention.

The hunger pangs stopped trying after a while, frustrated by their inability to get my attention.

One telling sentence, by the way, was your: "I don't think I really have <u>true</u> emotions." Of course not having true emotions is crap. Everyone has them; it's just not everyone can face up to and deal with them. I suppose there are worse weaknesses. But I've always seen you as someone who, for now, can't stop playing at life as a game. It isn't because you're *cold and hard and worldly, but rather because of all the opposite reasons.*

As protective guardians go, he could be a little harsh. But he was right. I did have emotions. They had been snuffed out, stuffed away in a closet whose contents were about to fall on my head. I hadn't been raised in absolute silence like Danny, but words were far from meaningful in our home. There was a clear pattern of denial of the obvious (no, your father does not in fact have a drinking problem), to be followed by an admission of the obvious (by the way, about your father), but only after a life-changing decision had already been made: your father is going into the Care Unit. You'll see him shuffling around in a bathrobe and slippers in the hospital, he may be crying. Then a new denial of the obvious (no, we do not in fact have marriage problems), followed by an admission of the obvious (by the way, about the marriage), but only after a life-changing decision had already been made: we are getting a divorce. That's how things were set up; my parents only admitted the problem they had denied all along when a decision had already been made without our input, a decision that would irrevocably change our lives. That means that there was always a discrepancy between what I *saw* to be true and what my parents *said* was true. (No

My feelings stopped trying after a while, frustrated by their inability to get my attention.

wonder I looked in the mirror and saw a fat chick.) That taught me to distrust my instincts, to ignore my emotions because they must be wrong. It became easy to dismiss my feelings; they stopped trying after a while, frustrated by their inability to get my attention.

I was sorry to see you verify the rumor about your parents. To me, any divorce is sad. I've been through two-other people's, mind you. And I hated it. I disagree with your statement about 20 years of marriage and not being happy, so end it. First, you may be (& probably are) strong, but what about your younger sisters? Don't they deserve a normal family until they're out of high school, too? And as for happiness—pooh! What is happiness but unconsciousness. A couple of six packs can take care of that. Why do all people live with happiness as their goal?

The "couple of six packs" comment was a jab at my new college pastime. "How is your drinking problem?" he had asked one night on the phone. The drinking was partly assimilation into the college subculture, partly a way to dampen the new emotions rushing to the surface. The loss of control that comes with intoxication was familiar to me, almost comforting, not because it made me think of my father (who was a quiet drunk), but because it re-created what it was like to be back at home. My sisters and I had no control, not only in the decision making, but over our own perceptions; we were made to distrust what was filtered through our own senses. Why I would want to replicate that feeling is an issue for another session. But even sick homes can make you homesick.

That doesn't mean my sisters and I didn't try to resist the family code, didn't try to anchor ourselves to something tangible, to find some sense of control. I learned early on that what I could control, perhaps the only thing I could control, was the food that went into my mouth. I could measure it, I could count its calories, I could limit it. I could trust the objectivity of the large black numbers on the bathroom scale, the red needle swinging ever backward. There is something sad and ironic about trying to prove you exist and matter by gradually disappearing, by making yourself into a ghost. But despite the carefully calculated portions, the excessive exercise, the empirical evidence on the scale, I saw no difference when I looked into the mirror. The offending curves were still there. The same silhouette stared back. The "interfering flesh" was still fleshy. Of course the truth was that I was dwindling away to nothing, but my mind had become a fun-house mirror. I literally saw what wasn't there. The by-product of being groomed to not see what is there.

Now I was in college becoming a lush just like my father; that's not the healthiest way to process emotions about your dad's alcoholism. But it wasn't so much my dad's drinking as the changes that came when it stopped. Everything shifted. My father had taken an honest look at his life; the assessment that came out of his mouth matched the situation, which was dismal. That wasn't a welcomed change. The family mechanism couldn't function with a little truth thrown in, it got stuck in the wheels, brought the whole thing to a crashing halt. No wonder I detached from my environment. No wonder I kept my secret a secret, at least until I left the home that required it.

The fact that I was making a case for the mutual happiness of my parents in my letter to John, spinning the story just as it had been spun to me, meant I was still partly in the dark. That's what we had been told: everything will be better now for you girls because your father and I will be happy. But at least the door had been opened, a little light had seeped in. John knew I would feel the pain of the divorce someday; it just wouldn't be *that* day. One neurosis at a time, please.

"I'm a firm believer in the Somerset Maugham clubfoot fraternity out of *Of Human Bondage*," another of his letters began, during this same time. I had to remind him I already belonged to the secret sorority of anorexics.

To be truly great, you've got to have a reason, not because wisdom comes from suffering (though it can) or you have to see black to understand white, but for a far more Freudian reason. Something in your life has to be out of kilter before you start asking questions, probing answers, tearing the world apart. People who are cozy are not going to go out looking for better blankets. Maybe your struggle with anorexia was your initial stimulant to thought and maybe having dealt with that is like having surgery on your clubfoot. God forbid we should sit back and find we have enough blankets someday.

I *was* tearing the world apart, or at least the internal stuff jammed into my closet. By now John knew, better than anyone, the sordid details of my eating disorder. He was trying to give meaning to my struggle, calling it my stimulant to thought, taking away the shame of a life out of kilter. He was also saying that not all greatness has to be goaded; sometimes it's simply the result of overcoming pain.

But my secret went deeper than John knew. It was a perfect storm of wanting to be perfect (although it could be argued that my perfectionism was another attempt at controlling the uncontrollable), a budding body and leering teachers,

It was a perfect storm of wanting to be perfect.

and a home that was broken before it was "broken." My sisters chose other avenues of resistance, more traditionally self-destructive ones, which is why my dad said I was the one kid they never worried about. Of course my actions were destructive, too, but they were also socially acceptable, even socially enviable. I had three college scholarships and jeans from the boys department to show for it.

The point here is that few people really know what they're living for. You and I don't either—I guess is the real point—but we're at least trying to find out…of course then, we probably wouldn't be if we'd have had warmer blankets. (We're really going to have to speak to our parents about those blankets.)

With wisdom comes some degree of sadness if for no other reason than with

*wisdom comes the knowledge of what you
can't do. And there are things you can't
do, Amy Amazing.*

I was too young to believe there were things I couldn't
do, and to prove my progress I wrote a long paper for one of
my classes. In it I bared my soul, examined all the stuff that
had fallen out of my closet with the wealth of insight one
psychology class afforded. But it was a start. And it was the
first time in my life I was willing to admit that what John said
about me might be true: maybe I wasn't cold and hard and
worldly, but rather the opposite.

*Everything you wrote about in your letter
made me happy-your journal, your
thinking, the fact that you saved my
letter to read last (!) but most of all the
long quote from your paper. I'll never
say you're shallow again-ever. I couldn't
believe you'd written it. You said about
yourself what I'd always thought about your
writing, beautifully constructed but little
depth. You wrote Mrs. B. papers-all the*

bullshit phrased beautifully, but not an iota of individuality. But this paper was just perfect, just perfect. Amy, baby, you just may be a writer after all.

But I didn't want to be a writer. I wanted to be a shrink. Like Danny, like Freud. Still I was happy John had acknowledged a change in me, that I had gone from beautiful B.S. to individuality. My emotions had gotten my attention, and I was just beginning the long process of sorting through them. But sadly something else was about to end: my love affair with Freud. He had become such an important part of my life that I had a portrait of him hanging on my dorm room wall, one drawn by my own hand, half of his face, appropriately, in the shadows. But the turner of my head now caused it to spin. I remember the day perfectly. It was a rainy afternoon, and I was sitting alone in the library, again, poring over another of Freud's original works. I was moving hungrily from page to page, eating up every word. Then I stumbled upon this statement: a woman's function, my esteemed mentor was saying, is simply and purely sexual. I stared at the page for a moment. Then I closed the book, sat quietly, listened as my idol crashed into pieces at my feet. Freud, it turned out, had been after my breast buds all along. His portrait came off the wall. God in Vienna had failed me.

Growing Up

Sorting through the stuff in my Fibber McGee's closet did bring some peace, the peace John saw as "most important" in that beautiful excerpt from his letter that opens this chapter. Maybe Emily Dickinson never left her room because she didn't need warmer blankets. Or maybe she was able to get things to fall into place on paper, on the little booklets she sewed to-gether to hold her poetry, like John's homemade graduation gift of words. But that's not all he had said in that letter. He had added one more condi-tion to achieving peace: "Neither Emily Dickinson nor I had or will have perfect peace. I think it's some-thing you are constantly building. Perhaps for peace we need at least one other person in our lives who really knows us."

"Perhaps for peace we need at least one other person in our lives who really knows us."

There were other stimulating exchanges during this period in our relationship that didn't center on Freud. After I read the play *Butley* for one of my English classes, I wrote John about the story, an English professor entangled with a young man, his former star pupil. "I must admit I'd like to read *Butley*," he wrote back. "It sounds hysterical, though I don't see why you'd have to be male to make it true for us. I'm sure the author wouldn't mind a little sexual change, if it still hung on the right plot." He wanted to reconfigure the play to accommodate us, to make us its principal participants, again assuming the roles

of fictional characters. "I'll go find the play over Christmas."
He did and then wrote an entire letter to me as if he were Butley. There were the endless, almost maternal, admonitions
against the devil's drink: "Can you be so stupid to think that
there's any worth in going out every night, in getting drunk
every weekend? Don't look at this as a fanatical Carrie Nation
starting up. It isn't just the drinking." There were chastise-
ments about relationships: "Still, with all that said, you do
seem to 'tire' of beaus rather quickly. I've said before that once
you've 'caught' the guy, you've lost interest. You're more inter-
ested in the chase than the capture. Of course, that could simply be because you're a virgin, and what *is* there to do after the
chase is over?" This went on for a while, he the wise sage dis-
pensing life advice, equipping the protagonist on the hero's
journey that began when she left the homeland.

But eventually we leveled out as equals when we realized
intimacy doesn't flourish in uneven soil. We were no longer
teacher and student, no longer Freud and Jung, no longer
Butley and his young lover, just John and Amy. A few years
later, when he opened the door to his own exploding closet,
he worried I had outgrown him, worried that we were uneven
again. He said so in a letter, poignantly, after admitting his
faults, after his own soul baring. He ended the letter with a
somber wish:

I hope our relationship survives your
growing up and my growing down.

He meant my growing up in the past tense, he said, and his growing down in the present, as a person I didn't recognize came tumbling out of his closet. He wondered if another of my idols had come crashing to the ground. Had he failed me?

But by now it was too late. I couldn't close his book and walk away. I had someone in my life I couldn't fool.

4

THE SPEAR CLOSET

Where the Weapons Are Stored

*You must avoid disagreements with boys,
even if they are wrong. It is always a problem
with the boys who want to disagree with you.
You must avoid them, too. When you get older
you will know how to manage I am sure.*
—TYPED LETTER FROM MY GRANDFATHER
WHEN I WAS TWELVE

I learned about John's secret at the end of our first year of letter writing. It did not come tumbling out of the closet, pulling everything on its head, like mine did. It slipped out sideways, almost an afterthought, in the middle of an argument. *Middle* is more descriptive than literal here, since we were arguing via post. I'm sure we made more progress than if we had been face-to-face; arguing by mail made it harder to storm out of the room or hang up the phone. Or hurl pointy objects.

My grandfather wrote letters to me for many years, too, and I always wrote him back, up until the time he died. He preserved all of my letters, along with carbon copies of his to me, in a manila folder in his basement office, his writing room. A family member gave me the folder full of letters when he died. Today you can barely read the faded handwriting on the label that simply says AMY. His advice about boys was evoked by a story in one of my letters. A boy began to beat me up at school, I had written, and I ran into the restroom. Then someone told another boy about the incident, and he started to beat up the boy who had been beating me up. The teacher said it was my fault; the fight started, she insisted, because I was boy-crazy. (In reality, she should have kept a better eye on her fellow teachers.) My grandfather bestowed his paternal advice, siding with my teacher, insisting that it was my responsibility to avoid disagreements with boys, with the hope that I would manage when I was older.

I was older now and still arguing with boys—or one boy, who happened to be a man. Even that was open to question. "I've always thought of myself intellectually as a genius, but with the emotions of a thirteen-year-old girl," John confessed in one of his letters. I was no match for his mind (he once dubbed me "intellectually plastic"), but for the most part it was an even match emotionally. My recent break from detachment put me at around the same emotional age. Hence the catfight.

The Spear Closet

Spear closet is an architectural term and an apt metaphor for the series of exchanges that marked the next stage in our relationship. The phrase applies to any leftover space in the design of a building or home that is too small to be of any real value. The only thing the space can really accommodate is something tall and thin, like a spear. Of course no one really stores spears, but it is a colorful way to describe dead space. It's also a colorful way to describe those times when John and I collided. It's interesting that the oldest usage of the word that gave us *closet* included not only the idea of a close encounter but one that involved conflict. Close, as in close enough to tear each other apart. John and I were both armed with our weapon of choice, the pen being mightier than the sword. Or spear.

It's not as if John had never uttered a harsh word to me before this time, or me to him. (He always reminded me that my initial reaction to him as a teacher was "disdain.") But all of his previous blistering had been chastisement, the kind of rebuke an authority figure metes out. Chastisement is uneven; you don't censure a peer. Anger is equal. Anger meant we

We were moving forward, even while collecting the shards left by our clumsy, sometimes brutal, attempts to unmask each other.

were moving forward, painfully, even while collecting the

shards left by our clumsy, sometimes brutal, attempts to unmask each other.

It started out as good-natured competition. Instead of
the advice being handed down, from mentor to protégée, the
admonitions went back and forth, laterally. There was a spirited exchange of ideas—points and counterpoints—with
plenty of needling but no spearing. We were each other's
chief opponent and biggest cheerleader. For a time it was a
perpetual pep rally.

I had to laugh when I read your last
letter and you said my jogging was in
competition to all your jock boyfriends.
From reading your letter, I'd say I was
competing with you. It's almost like we're
trying to see who can outdo the other in
accomplishing things and growing
mentally. Fortunately, it isn't a petty
competitiveness. I got such a kick out of
reading your letter (as well as the
envelope). You sound so good and so alive
and so Amy. I really did miss you when I

read it. But I was so happy you were alive and thinking and doing.

I just reread your last letter and again I'm struck by the irony of both of us out there living our lives so-forcefully. I think even if we find out we were wrong to do all this-at some point in the future-we'll still feel justified in having tried it. God, we both sound like Norman Vincent Peale! But it's important. It's good we have each other.

I'm sure he felt that way at the time. But soon my being "so Amy" would be the very thing to divide us; it would put us at twenty paces, armed not with foils but with spears.

We All Wear Masks

Now to return to our philosophy corner,
Demian.

He had already compared me to Danny Saunders in *The Cho-sen,* reworked the play *Butley* to make it fit our male–female genders; now he was calling me Demian. He was not refer-ring to the scary demon-child in *The Omen* films, but the title character of a Hermann Hesse novel, the one with three naked people and a sparrow hawk on the cover. I'm not sure why John called me Demian.

If anything I was Sinclair, the novel's narrator, who re-counts stories of his friend Demian rescuing him time and time again. Demian is otherworldly, a societal outcast, direct-ing Sinclair on his path to self-awareness. The name Demian comes from the word *daemon,* which can mean a guiding spirit or even a ghost, a visitant. It is Demian who sees through Sinclair, who keeps Sinclair from becoming a drunk when he's away at school. He is more than a sobriety broker, though; Demian shows up in times of crisis, a guardian spirit, who teaches Sinclair to trust his own instincts. Even when they are not together, Sinclair can feel Demian's influence on his thinking, his actions, can feel his presence in his dreams. This influence continues until Sinclair matures, is finally at peace, and then Demian's presence must withdraw. Sinclair doesn't tell the story, which covers ten years of his life until early adulthood, as it is happening. He waits until he is older, until he has the time and space and opportunity to reflect on the stages of his personal development and Demian's impact on them. He is looking back with the clarity that comes from being both separate and distant, looking back on the most important relationship of his life.

"We all wear masks and some of them should be kept."

Now to return to our philosophy corner, Demian. You can take the mask idea one step further and see why I put so little in relationships. If each person wears a mask to himself and also to others, it's practically impossible (except by chance) to have a "good" relationship with someone else. Even if you do get through the mask they wear in public, you've only gotten to the person they think they are. So actually, you'll never get to the real person and be able to react to it because he doesn't know what it is. Of

course, them who needs to have a "good"
relationship. Kurt Vonnegut wrote, "We
all wear masks and some of them
should be kept."

I have tried to confirm the source of this quote but found
it impossible to link it to Kurt Vonnegut. What Kurt Vonnegut did say was "Be careful what you pretend to be because
you are what you pretend to be." The opposite of what John
was saying. But John didn't really mean it either. He wanted
a "good" relationship. Saying he didn't was another mask. A
mask he wore as a teacher, too. One day in English class,
after ritualistically applying his ChapStick (I've never seen
him without a thin layer of wax on his lips), he climbed atop
his soapbox and began to preach. It didn't matter that he was
irreligious; he could be judgmental, and that day he was
downright Pecksniffian. (He would both love and hate that I
called him this. Love because the word is based on a character from a Dickens novel, hate because the character is ob-
noxiously pious.) His sermon topic: love. He insisted there
was no such thing as "real love"; it was a fantasy, an illusion.
Love was nothing more than two people using each other to
get their needs met. It was selfish, if you looked at it emotionally; or a simple contract of reciprocation, if you looked
at it biologically. That's what he told a roomful of hormonal
teenagers. No teacher talked like that at our school, not even
the biology teacher, deconstructing enduring themes of love

into Darwinian survival skills. But he needed to be careful what he was pretending to be.

> I agree with Kurt Vonnegut. Everyone is so pathetic-to me the hermit non-socializer-that it would be morbid to see under all those masks. Without the restraint of those masks, we'd have people [dancing] in the streets. It isn't society so much that restrains people as the persona society has forced upon most people. Maybe Hell's Angels are more real than Boston socialites!

For a time our philosophy corner was just as it sounded, cozy and cerebral. But then we stopped talking about concepts in general and started applying them specifically, personally—on behalf of the other person. "I love the mask you say I wear," he wrote, "that I hide behind my sarcasm, that I use it to appear 'indifferent,' as if I 'don't give a damn.' Is that really how you perceive me? What a hell of an actor I am!" That *is* the way I perceived him. Later he took on a writing project that required him to describe himself in the third person. First he gave an outsider's view; a school administrator had called him "crude" and "obnoxious." Then he described himself as he saw himself: "He is a bundle of sensitivities, hidden by a brash, quick-witted exterior." That's exactly what I said, brash on the outside, gooey on the inside. A genius with the emotions of a thirteen-year-old girl.

He was a genius with the emotions of a thirteen-year-old girl.

I do think a person can pretty well get in touch with his "real self." However, I don't think most people do. The problem is one of pronouns: they don't know themselves, but I do.

I know you think I'm really egotistical, but actually you're wrong. That's all a mask. I'm very shy but I refuse to let that stop me or hinder me in any way. But, I do think I'm better than anyone else, not that that's saying much.

He was not egotistical, but he was better than anyone else. That was his defense. "And since fair is fair, should I describe the mask I see you to wear—Amy Amazing, who pretends she can do everything?" It was the old laundry list: I was shallow, self-centered, a drunkard. I think by then he realized I had tuned out the familiar litany so he devised a new strategy, comparing me to a girl at my high school who was grossly overweight, whose bad skin was legendary, who wore glasses thicker than mine (before I got contacts).

> You're nothing more than... [the poor girl's name]... you just had all the breaks. You were better looking, had a better figure, better personality, better raised, etc. So you're just her with fate on your side... kind of hard to feel good about yourself now, isn't it?

He was baiting me, of course, having moved past the pleasantries, positioning his spear. It was mean to compare me—someone who was mortified of gaining weight—to the fattest girl in school. If he was goading me to greatness, he was doing so by needling my deepest insecurities. I thought he was being entirely too generous with himself, entirely too hard on me. I shot back that he was again hiding behind his cynicism, that I was certain there was turmoil seething beneath his smug mask.

> Oh, so there's a "world of turbulence" beneath my mask? There are some fears

behind my mask-most well grounded, quite
necessary-and a lot of anger-ditto
grounded-and one or two desires I wouldn't
want to get around-pity the poor sheep-but a
world of turbulence? No, I've got too solid
a base for that.

He had too solid a base for that. As opposed to me, the broken girl from the broken home.

Side Trips into the Bizarre

Once he had finished likening me to the student he called the White Whale (one literary comparison I could have done without), he moved on to see how I fared next to his friend; she, too, had a solid base. "When I look at my best friend and compare her to you . . ." This again seemed unfair since I was eighteen at the time, and she was his age. How could I compete with his lifelong best friend? ". . . what you're missing of importance is a solid background. You tell your mother I said this and I'll never speak to you again."

My mother hearing this part of his letters should have been the least of his worries.

But that's what just hit me. My friend and I both come from <u>very</u> solid middle-class families and for all our oddities and side trips into the bizarre, at the core we're both very solid. Oh, I know you think I'm strange, and in many ways that are important to society but not to humanity I suppose I am. But all my (& her) peculiarities are safe because they're built on that proverbial "strong foundation."

Whether or not all his peculiarities were safe was still to be decided. What seemed certain was my fate. I was on shaky ground, now and for the rest of my life, because my parents had chosen to end their marriage. It seemed cruel for him to bring this up while I was still processing my parents' divorce—well, not quite processing, but at least trying to accept it. I didn't tell any of my college friends that my parents were divorcing, not even my roommate. It didn't have to be known in my new world. (The old world still required secrets.) The next year when a steady boyfriend flew home with me to meet my family, I told him my parents were divorced just before we boarded the plane. He didn't need to know before that moment. I was too ashamed.

My mom told me about the divorce over the phone. I had called to ask if there was any money in the family budget for me to pledge a sorority. I'm sure I already knew the answer. My college was completely paid for by an academic scholarship or else I would have been stuck at home attending the city college. But I thought if she knew that several sororities were wooing me, the misplaced Midwesterner—I could be the novelty sister, a surefire conversation-starter at any mixer—she would find a way. Mom was unbending, and we began to argue. Finally she blurted out there was no money in the family budget, especially now that she and my father were getting a divorce. That's how I found out. It slipped out sideways, almost an afterthought, in the middle of an argument. No sorority, no money, no more family. The trial separation was over; the verdict, divorce. The spoils of war were already being divided (and my dad was the big loser): my mother was in the process of moving back into the family home, my dad into his own apartment. When I went away to college, my dad and younger sisters were at home—the same sisters John had made a case for, saying they deserved a normal family until they were out of high school. (They would never get a normal family, even

> *It slipped out sideways in the middle of an argument. No sorority, no money, no more family.*

if my parents had stayed together.) When I returned at
Christmas, my mom had moved back in and my dad was out.
True to code, the family arrived cheerily, as a single unit, to
greet me at the airport in December. I wonder if I ate at all
over that break.

I didn't cry when my mom blurted out that she and my
father were getting a divorce. The only time I remember crying was when Dad (another frequent letter-sender) wrote me
to say our dog, a casualty of the divorce, had died on the
"farm" they sent him to. (His apartment building didn't allow
pets, and my mom didn't like animals.) I cried when our dog
died, but not when the marriage died. Of course my emotional allocation was unhealthy, even odd, but I could afford
to be odd, peculiar, a hermit non-socializer, John was saying,
if only I had the strong foundation he did.

You see, I would rather my parents went
on pretending to love each other than get
a divorce, but I never had to worry about
it. My parents were from the no-divorce
generation. The thought never crossed our
minds-solidity, again. And, Amy my dear-
reader of Freud-you tell me what it
means when a girl says she needs her

*mom more than her dad and that her
mom is her support. Of course, you can't
be blamed for any of it.*

Any more than I could take credit for having a better life
than the White Whale. I must have lauded my parents for
their honesty in not pretending to love each other anymore;
of course, it was spin and John should have been used to it
by now. Instead he countered by saying he would never have
to worry about that; if need be, his parents would go on pretending. If he were a child, he could have said it in sing-
song—nah-nah-nah-nah-nah—for all its sophistication. My
defense, at least then, was that I only needed one parent anyway. I sided with my mom, the one who had repositioned
herself at the family home, along with the rest of my sisters.
It's possible John was trying to provoke me into expressing
the "true emotions" I thought eluded me; if so, he was in
luck. I don't have my exact words back to him, but I do know
they included a wish for his eternal damnation.

I knew you and P. [my latest boyfriend]
*wouldn't last by the by-says something. And
wasn't your "you can go to hell as far as
your comment about my family and my
lack of solidarity go" comment just a bit*

much. Bye-bye P. only seems to further illustrate my point there. Besides, you shouldn't take philosophical points so personally. My god! You'd think I'd personally attacked your family or something! "Go to hell" indeed!

I shouldn't take his philosophical points so personally, he said. No child of divorce considers the issue philosophical. Distance from pain always makes it easier to explain, to deconstruct. You can't preach about divorce—any more than you can preach about love—if you haven't experienced it. Now that we were inside the spear closet, there was no lingering sentiment of the former days: "I hope you realize you can always write about the down things, too." Hardly.

Now that we were inside the spear closet, there was no lingering sentiment of the former days.

I have noted that one of the first signs of maturity is being able to look critically at one's family. It deals with being able to see <u>both</u> Mommy and Daddy aren't perfect and then goes on from there.

My laundry list had expanded from shallow, self-centered, and a drunkard to now include touchy and immature. He continued to link my string of beaus (as he called them) with my newly fractured home.

> I really think you'll have to calm down some ("mellow out") before you'll have a solid relationship with anyone, if you ever do. I don't think you're shallow intellectually, though you tend to be a little plastic there at times, but I do think you're shallow emotionally. People just don't react to their parents' divorce as you did, for example.
>
> When was the last time you told your father you loved him, and kissed him?
>
> Here's what I really think about you: you're just too f-ing afraid to keep up a relationship with someone.

He was wrong about that, just as wrong as when he told me I didn't have the patience to write a book. It turned out my most enduring relationship with a man had been with him. He was right about something else, though: there was a lot of anger under his mask.

The Secret

John had a secret beneath his secret, like someone who takes off a disguise only to reveal another disguise underneath. When I said he revealed his first secret as an aside, I mean that literally: he put the revelation in parentheses, it was so incidental to him. He was angry at me, flailing at me in a letter, and then, exhausted by the effort, he put down his pen, sheathed his spear. He didn't have the energy to bother with me anymore. He probably wouldn't have finished or even sent that letter if his phone hadn't rung at just that moment.

It was late afternoon in early April my freshman year when I read the letter he didn't intend to send. Before class, I dug all of my letters out of my slender dorm mailbox. I received so many letters that year. I cut out the addresses of each letter-sender and put them in a scrapbook of my college years. John's address is there, too, pasted to the page. There is nothing that stands out about it, no indication that his would be the only letters I kept. I always saved his letters to read last, and I always read them privately. My college friends took note of this, another reason to accuse us of having an affair. I put his letter in my backpack, took it to class with me to read afterward, a reward for having sat through a too-long lecture. (He used to save my letters as a reward after jogging.) After class I found a spot on the steps outside the classroom building, not wanting to go too far, to waste any more time. I remember the day perfectly. It was one of the first days of springlike weather, the kind that makes you feel suspended in time. I closed my eyes, face up to the sun. It was almost a ritual, getting prepared to read one of his letters. I was willing away the drone of the professor I had just left, like a ceremonial washing before entering the temple. But today there would be no veneration. We had been arguing, and the letter began with a defense against some accusation I had made. And then:

> *I was willing away the drone of the professor I had just left, like a ceremonial washing before entering the temple.*

You see me as a cynic, which I am. But (and remember how I believe in paradox) I'm also quite capable of deep and abundant emotions. I have no respect for men who can't appreciate or feel poetry and music...and people. I've been blessed with never having to worry about my *masculinity or sexuality. (I've always known I was gay!)*

I stared at the page for a moment. Then I folded up the letter, sat quietly.

"There are aspects of me we've never covered," he explained later. "You said you regretted that it took me so long to stop hiding behind sarcasm. Amy! You were fifteen when I met you! Tell me you think an adult teacher should be perfectly honest with a fifteen-year-old student?!"

I wasn't upset or angry or disappointed. But I was confused. Of course I had heard the rumors in high school. Most attractive thirty-year-old men at that time were married, especially in education where there's no shortage of women. But I never believed them. I always defended him, stood up for him, offered our engagement as evidence. Then there was all the sexual content in his letters to me, half of which I didn't understand at the time. (He was considerate enough to insert exclamation marks enclosed in parentheses after the bawdiest comments so that the joke wouldn't slip past me, but I've taken most of the exclamation marks out of his letters.) Why try so hard—now that I was out of high school—to paint himself as a red-blooded American male? A red-blooded American male who wrote in blue: parts of his novel, which he read to me over the phone, included passages that were lewd, and the object of the lechery was a character modeled after me. In one letter he asks me to book our motel room for when he visits me. I read the innuendos now—I'm spinning the story again, they were too direct to be innuendos—and I think, *Where were my parents?* Then I remember: they were busy being happy.

It wasn't just our private letters. When we were discussing *A Tale of Two Cities* in his class in high school, I was the only student who understood what the Evrémonde character was up to. I didn't want to say out loud that he had kept the poor peasant woman as a sex slave, so I stumbled, and surprise, surprise, spun it a little by saying he kept her for his own pleasure, for his pastime. John loved this. "His pastime?" he shouted. "You mean like a hobby? Like collecting stamps? What did he do, lick her?" He was proud I had caught the intent of what Dickens was implying to his pious nineteenth-century audience, but prouder still to mercilessly embarrass me in front of a classroom of contemporaries.

There was another teacher in our school whom everyone thought was gay, who was too meticulous with his clothes, who lisped and gasped. (The Hollywood caricature before there was one.) But John was not like that at all. A friend had told him that it was a good thing he wasn't too good looking because he could get into a lot of trouble with his mouth. He was provocative; he attracted women. There were girls at my high school in love with him.

He told me he was gay in a letter he never intended to send.

❧

He told me he was gay in a letter he never intended to send. Not because he didn't want me to know his secret, but because he wasn't sure he wanted to bother with me anymore.

Why Bother?

When I graduated from college three years later, there was no homemade booklet of quotes, carefully chosen and typed, no magazine photos pasted to every page. Instead John sent me a single quote scrawled on the back of notebook paper. It was by Anne Morrow Lindbergh and began, "This is the pit . . . I am in it. I am alone. I am abandoned. There is no one and nothing to help me." That was his graduation gift to me. "There is power in words," he wrote in the margin. But even his handwriting seemed tired, ghostlike.

It wasn't because he decided not to bother with me anymore that there was such a difference between his two graduation gifts. Because he did. He bothered for college and six years beyond college. But there was something else going on with him at the time, the secret beneath his secret.

He decided to bother with me because I was the one who called him on the phone the night he was ready to give up on me.

Hate me if you like (indeed you do seem to have a "ping pong" problem there), but I *think I judge people more on their reactions to lost dog stories than on their intelligence. I never totally trust anyone who didn't have their own pet as a child.*

I did have my own pet as a child. My dog had just died on a "farm." My reaction was to cry.

I have the terrible feeling that they could accidentally push me off a cliff and not feel too bad about it. Being pushed off the cliff isn't so bad-after all, it was an accident. But I would want to be mourned.

Would you mourn for me, Amy? I think probably not. I sincerely hope it's just youth and not a permanent affliction with you, but I have serious reservations.

It was youth. It wasn't a permanent affliction. Would I mourn him? Twenty years have passed, and I'm writing a book about him. I'm doing what Sinclair did for Demian and for the same reason: ours was the most important relationship in my life. That's why John was Demian, not me. That's why John is still Demian.

As soon as I heard your voice I knew I would still bother.

Believe it or not, that's as far as I got when you called. Surrealistic. You forced me to think. I really was feeling "Amy, oh well, why bother." But as soon as I heard your voice I knew I would still bother.

Well, it's the next morning and time to end all this.

I didn't know he was on the verge of giving up on me. My phone call was not a preemptive strike. I don't know what prompted me to call at the moment of decision; sometimes I felt his influence even when we weren't together. I don't know what I said or what in my voice soothed his wrath.

There was a cease-fire. But the Ping-Pong problem was not just mine. Soon we were fighting again, tearing away at each other's masks.

You know, sometimes I think I prefer writing you rather than talking to you.

There's an awful lot of surface to you to get through to get to the real element of Amy. I know you think I'm always telling you you're shallow, but actually I'm not. I think what I'm usually trying to say is that you act shallow. You neatly hide most of the real Amy away. I suppose I just don't always like what you hide it with.

He was moving into position.

You're one of those very intelligent people whose minds work on overdrive. You have ambition—that's important.

But I think somehow you work best on paper.

The spear had hit its mark.

My grandfather had warned me not to argue with boys. He told me to avoid them, even if they are wrong. But this time there was no restroom to run into. No one to take up my cause. I was being blamed again. Maybe this time it really was my fault.

He had written it down for the record, in black and

white: you work best on paper. It wasn't just an assessment from my English teacher. It was a judgment from the one person who knew me.

I fought back, but I didn't win. In the end it wasn't even close. His weapons, his words were more powerful, more piercing. He had said that what first attracted him to me was that we both loved literature, were both good with words, "English things." That was it, really: what connected us, from the very beginning, were words. What *kept* us together, he said, was something more complex. But he had changed his mind.

He would still bother. But now he only wanted us to be together on paper.

Necessary Armor

Last night, after writing this ending, I had a dream about John. He was a visitant, like Demian. In the dream he came to see me, and we began working together. We were lecturing, touring another country together. He even spent time with my family; not my husband and kids, but the family I grew up with. While we were traveling abroad, I went into a bookstore and found a first edition of the famously orange-covered *Catcher in the Rye*. Next to it was his favorite if less popular Salinger book, *Franny and Zooey*. I bought a copy for him. It was a time of seamless joy; we were perfectly in sync. And then on the last night, out of sequence, out of character with the visit, he insulted me. He insulted me at a restaurant, in front of my family. He said it matter-of-factly, like he always did. He wasn't comparing me to the White Whale, but it was along those lines. What he said wasn't even true. Why would he ruin our visit with a hurtful remark like that?

When I woke up I thought, *I want to remember everything about the visit but that moment*. But that moment was the most important part, the most important clue. That's when I understood. We were getting too close. He was getting uncomfortable. He had to create distance at the end of our wonderful visit together. I had it all wrong. I had closed the door on the spear closet too soon, wrapped up the chapter with the wrong ending. The anger of this time in our relationship, this real time I call the spear closet, did not make us equals. We clearly weren't. I saw the anger as a sign of us becoming more intimate, and it was, but not in the way I thought. It was a sign of us becoming more intimate because it triggered John's defense against intimacy. That's why his letters were so uneven, so cruel. It didn't make sense, since he was reversing the warm affection and concern, even contradicting the content of earlier letters.

After he told me he considered himself a genius intellectually but with the emotions of a thirteen-year-old girl, he added one more condition: "I wear the necessary armor. Perhaps you should, too."

He put on the necessary armor when we started to get too close. That's why he visited me last night. I had gotten it all wrong. The anger wasn't the next step in my becoming the one other person in his life who really knew him; it was his way of making sure that never happened.

He put on the necessary armor when we started to get too close.

Author's Note: Something strange happens to me when I enter the spear closet, when I revisit John's angry letters. For the longest time I couldn't pinpoint it. It's almost as if two people are telling the story, but they're not me and John. Or I'm on a seesaw, but it's not John who is on the other end. Instead I'm in both seats, teetering between myself now and myself then. I am confidently explaining our relationship at one point; then suddenly I am a hurt and defensive teenager. My voice cracks. My word choice becomes less sophisticated. My thinking less clear. His cutting words have made me a child again. John's words hurt me, but it is not just hurt I feel. Something else is at work here. As I continue writing about our relationship, what that is becomes clear. Then I have to make a decision about whether I can finish telling our story, whether we can be together at all, even on paper.

5

RAIN IN THE STORE-CLOSET

What It Takes to Write

There's nothing more disheartening than being on the
fifth page of something that's supposed to be a novel.

—JOHN

I appreciate your trusting me enough to write such a personal paper. I like the structure, that you began and ended
it with a letter." That's what Dr. Reed had written at the top of
my in-class theme during the spring semester. I just found the
paper this afternoon. I don't even remember writing it. My
son had asked me to dig through my college papers to see if it
was *Steppenwolf* or *Siddhartha* that had changed my life when
I was his age. How terrible that I can't remember which Hermann Hesse novel changed my life. After overturning the box
that contained the few things I saved from college (the journals, of course, are gone), I saw the paper for Dr. Reed and
was surprised that "Dear Amy" was the opening sentence.

Dr. Reed assigned an in-class theme once a week to his freshman Honors English class. Most students brought in old papers they had written in high school to recopy onto loose-leaf paper. Dr. Reed didn't care; he was giving us all A's, he said,

He was my high school Honors English teacher. I hated him.

since we wouldn't have made it into the program if we hadn't been A students to start with. We were good for it, he told us on the first day of class. I never felt right about recycling high school papers, so on this day I must have brought in some of John's letters to write about our relationship.

I opened with an excerpt from John's letter, and then my eighteen-year-old self offered this exposition:

This is the first of a series of letters I receive every two weeks from the author of the unpublished [the name of John's finished novel] and the incomplete [the novel he was writing, with me as a character]. He was my high school Honors English teacher. I hated him. He wore pink shirts and purple ties with pointed boots. He was an excellent teacher, but he embarrassed me in class. I remember being forced to explain the rape scene in *A Tale of Two Cities* to the entire class because no one else realized it was a rape scene.

Yesterday when I added the story about John embarrassing me in class to the previous chapter, I didn't know I would find a description of it written by my eighteen-year-old self today. (Some guiding spirit must have led me to it.) I don't remember having written about John in college or having shared parts of his letters with Dr. Reed. I didn't know that the paper included my first reaction to his pointy-toed boots or that I hated him. "Perhaps he was handsome, perhaps I liked him, perhaps I also found him repulsive; I could not be sure of that either," says Sinclair of meeting Demian for the first time.

My junior and senior years of high school I was editor-in-chief of the school newspaper, and he was the advisor. The first year of our partnership was turbulent; we fought constantly.

We still fought constantly.

He asked me to marry him. He told all the freshmen that we were engaged. He claims he doesn't love me but I remember the look on his face the first time I walked into his classroom wearing my college T-shirt, purchased over spring break after a visit to the campus. He then realized where I'd be spending

the next four years. He bought me a class schedule
for the city college, and I bought him a guide to
apartment dwelling in [my college town].

The second page of the paper, which would have been
filled front and back, single-spaced, is missing. I can't find it
anywhere. (I wonder what I wrote.) The last page of the
paper is an excerpt from John's letter in which he stages our
reunion scene in front of his students: the pathos, the running to embrace each other, the cameras snapping photos.

It wasn't that way at all. I walked into the classroom,
and the book he was reading to his students
dropped from his hands to the floor. We have a
unique relationship even if it is limited to letters for
now. But as I am sure Samuel Richardson would
agree, there is much to be said for letters.

That's how I ended the paper. I had to look up who Samuel Richardson was. I didn't remember. I'm sure I was showing off for my professor with the reference, just as I must
have assumed that calling my pen pal an author would have
impressed him. Samuel Richardson had written a famous
novel that consisted almost entirely of letters written by one
character. To get to know the other characters in the book
you had to see them through this character's eyes, through
this character's letters. That's how I'm getting to know my

eighteen-year-old self, and even my present-day self. Through John's eyes, through John's letters.

I honored his wish. We were only together on paper.

Rain in the Store-Closet

We did of course see each other in person again, although not as often since the spear had hit its mark. The phone calls were less frequent. It was just the letters now.

The very last time I saw him was when he came to visit me at graduate school. I took him on a tour of the grounds at night, and under the starlit sky and in the perfect stillness of a sleeping campus, he said, "This is the worst thing you could have ever done to me." (I was there studying psychology instead of writing, but that's not what he was talking about.) Those were his last words to me in person, the last words we spoke face-to-face.

The very last time I saw him was when he came to visit me at graduate school.

I guess writing letters was fitting for two people first drawn together by "English things," as he said. Letters tell more about a person than almost anything; they're the next best thing to a diary, especially if you've destroyed all of yours. If it was the easiest way for him to deal with me, then I would have to accept that. The only record I have of myself during those years, except for a few college papers, are his letters. That's why I needed to get to know myself, my character, through his words. If he had decided not to bother with me anymore, I would have lost the best accounts, the most intimate accounts, of myself during that time. But he wasn't the only one experiencing weariness in the relationship. When I began to write with less fervor he thought I, too, might be giving up:

> I was wondering if the goodbye you ended your last letter with was meant to be continental, where goodbye means exactly what it says. How silly. Besides, I'd miss you.

We were both making concessions, adjusting to the changing relationship. Things got busy for me. I wasn't sitting alone in my dorm room writing letters to him night after night. More and more, I had to squeeze him in. That's why he said my mind was in overdrive, thought I wasted all my time on "frivolous social stimuli." In yet another tirade about why I'd never be a writer, he said, "You can't write in the middle of a bar. You can't write while you're dancing. You can't write if your spare time is all clogged up with frivolity." We were so different that way. He was a "hermit non-socializer"; he loved winter if just for the fact that it forced people to stay inside. He tried out new recipes alone, tended his garden alone, read poetry alone. I was an ever-flitting social butterfly, having been cocooned longer than most teenage girls. The students who attached themselves to him in high school were exactly like him. He made fun of the misfits but they lined up behind him, as if he were a pointy-toed Pied Piper. (*Pied* means multicolored, so that explains his pink shirts and purple ties.)

I was social in public high school, too—eventually. There were a few obstacles at first; I hadn't gone to public school with most of the kids enrolled in my high school, and the majority of my peers were starting at the Catholic high school. I won a scholarship to the Catholic high school, but my sister had some trouble there so two of my older sisters and I transferred to the public high school. (When I asked where the money had gone, my mom admitted that she'd used my scholarship money to buy my dad a baby-blue leisure suit and to pay tuition for my two younger sisters at my Catholic school.) Another of my obstacles to finding new friends, at least the right kind of friends, was guilt by association: I first had to disengage from the nerdy academics my classes lumped me together with. Our high school was like

You could be a jock and cool, you could even be a druggie and cool, but you could not be a nerd and cool.

any other, with social signatures of nerd, jock, druggie, or cool kid. You could be a jock and cool, you could even be a druggie and cool, but you could not be a nerd and cool. (Geek chic was decades away.)

I was able to gain admission into cool mostly through my physical transformation, by straightening the Afro, tossing the glasses, shedding the pounds. (No more ugly duckling, no more rough-edged cocoon.) Maybe I belonged on John's island of misfit toys at first, but by my sophomore year I was decidedly unfit, in a good way. No one would mistake me for Jesus in *Godspell*. I was still devoted to books, but I no longer looked the part. (Becoming pretty, John often reminded me, was what made me callous, like a person who has escaped quicksand but refuses to help others still sinking.) I don't know why John and I stayed connected; I had better things to do on Saturday nights than hang out at his home on Utopia Lane, although I sometimes did. Now that I had a higher social ranking, I was careful to disengage from (that is, ditch) the few friends I had scrounged up when I first started high school. My and John's attachment to each other, or why it continued past my transformation, was harder to explain than that of his usual band of outcasts, who were less changeable. He offered them a safe place to be odd, a refuge for peculiarity, utopia on Utopia Lane. But I was mainstream now. What did I still need from him? He would ask that question more than once.

After our stint in the spear closet, we were less transparent in our letters. At least for a time. We became self-conscious, embarrassed by the anger, by the attempts to pull off each other's masks. The masks would come off on their own with less violence, sadly and dramatically. Of course I didn't know then that his anger was an avoidance tactic; I only know it now because of the dream. But I did know things changed, because we weighed our words more carefully.

That's how we went from the spear closet to the store-closet, to rain in the store-closet. The phrase is, appropriately, from a letter Jane Austen wrote to her sister Cassandra. (I have to confess here that I am not a Jane Austen fan, although I would walk on glass for any of the three Brontë sisters.) Jane Austen admitted that knowing others besides her sister were reading her letters made her self-conscious; she was more likely to feel the need to liven her speech, to show off with her words: "I am looking about for a sentiment, an illustration, or a metaphor in every corner of the room. Could my ideas flow as fast as the rain in the store-closet, it would be charming." Angry winter weather had deluged their storage closet, causing it to collapse, allowing rain to pour in. Austen had found the metaphor she was looking for in the corner of her room: rain in the store-closet. While Austen may have been looking for illumination, for quick-wittedness, the most important thing I gleaned from her letter is that the audience changes the writer.

John was having trouble with his latest novel. That's a lot of what we wrote about in our letters during this time. "There's nothing more disheartening than being on the fifth page of something that's supposed to be a novel—except maybe being on page four, where I was for several days." But the real problem was not writer's block; it was that he was writing for an audience, and that changed him.

"Ah, the pieces of myself that I've found in my writing,"

John announced one day. But he was throwing those pieces away.

Dirt and Blood

I've only read excerpts from John's novels or heard them read over the phone. His great American novel never got published, although bits and pieces of it live on in his letters. I'm not surprised there were no takers. The novel was lofty and sanitized; and he, of course, was nei-

He did not get dirty, he did not open a vein.

ther. He distanced himself from himself in order to be An Author; he did not get dirty, he did not open a vein.

He embedded excerpts from his novel in his letters, and there the contrast was greatest: polished words surrounded by dirt and blood.

He complained that writing to me took him away from his real work. But the letters were his real work—his most compelling and purest writing—and The Novel, dear to his heart and oozing treacle, was the distraction. A friend of his told me John wanted to put together a book of letters they wrote to each other in college, but he rearranged and re-wrote the letters until they lost their meaning. He was writing for an audience. Knowing others were reading his college letters made him search the room for a sentiment, an illustration, or a metaphor, the way Jane Austen did, and the passages became extravagant, sentimental. That's what I thought of his novel writing, too. It's what literary critics call purple prose. The man in the purple tie writing purple prose.

It's always possible that he only sent me the flowery stuff—maybe there was only a purple patch or two, in the whole of a novel that was otherwise—but there was no mistaking the difference in style. Sometimes his words were too dressed up, dignified like, other times too mawkish, as if the brash, quick-witted exterior had receded, the genius relenting to the emotions of a thirteen-year-old girl.

It turns out then that the best account, the most intimate account, John had of himself during that time was his letters. When he was intentionally trying to express himself for an audience, he was too self-conscious, more suit and wing tips than pink shirt and pointy boots. He had in fact found pieces of himself in his writing, but all those pieces were in his letters. In them he was too busy yelling, exasperating, chastising, teaching, and doting to be self-conscious.

I think back to when I would have cut off my [arm] to get published, then how I would have liked the money and the fame, then the feeling of accomplishment to now-it would be kind of neat. I've come to see

accomplishment in a different light,
especially so now in my new life.
Accomplishment is writing the book; that's
something you've done. If it sells a lot of
copies, that's something someone else has
done. It might help explain this if you keep
in mind that I don't think much of
competitive sports.

But you can accomplish things for
others, I think. It's just that you can't
accomplish much for many and you should
settle in with what you can do.

He accomplished much for me. That's why I want to fold
our relationship into a book. Not the book he was never able
to get published, but a book of his true writings, the book
that should have been published in the first place.

John did see some of his writing in print during those
years. He posted evidence of it on the bulletin board in his
classroom. It was a letter to the editor of *Time* magazine. The
magazine published a brief excerpt from his long letter, and
in it he accused some political figure, probably the president,
of "blatant hypocrisy." I was so impressed by those two

words, so impressed by his accomplishment, to see his name in print. He was bolstered by the recognition, kept plugging away at the typewriter.

And I'm bloody proud of myself, if you can't tell. I've been doing great. I feel successful and I know I'm going to continue to be. I feel just like you sound. There's still a lot to think about and discover and there's a lot for me to accomplish yet—my writing among other things. So let's see who goes the furthest.

My money is on him.

Crash into My Car

My social schedule was not the only reason John thought I'd never be a writer. He compiled a list of other obstacles, and they were all personal shortcomings.

I couldn't sit still long enough; I was impatient.

Somehow I get this view of your being too busy, too antsy. I can't see you writing the great American novel; I don't think you have the patience.

I was a doer, an accomplisher, not an intellectual. I was incapable of deep thought.

Thinking and the amount of time spent thinking is my top priority trait—for an intellect. And I mean pure meditative contemplation. I'm sure you read all the right books, but what do you do with them when you're finished?

Despite the mounting evidence, every once in a while he saw a glimmer of hope in me, in my redemption as a person able to express herself. I sent him an account of my spending a weekend at the farm where my roommate's family lived.

Despite the mounting evidence, every once in a while he saw a glimmer of hope in me.

You keep writing letters like that and I may never be unhappy! Just the mental picture of you riding around on a motorcycle behind some farm boy is enough to keep me joyful all the way through the awful christmas season. And feeding corn you broke off the ear to the horses-what a lovely touch! You really ought to be a writer.

Now I have a reason to be.

Why I Write

John had finished his second, maybe third, novel. His regimen, when writing letters to me didn't interrupt it, was to write two hours each night after school, five nights a week. He started this schedule just as I started college.

All of this, I'm sure, is of very little interest to you, but as I was the means

of getting you out of reading your
anthropology assignment, you're getting me
out of working on a new novel. I've
finished the other novel. As for trying to
be published, I find it hard to make
myself do these kinds of things.

Perhaps a publisher will just crash
into my car or something.

I do view one of my greatest personality
accomplishments as getting rid of any
desire for fame, etc. How silly to want to
be known by a lot of unknown people. I
have, moreover, derived a great deal of
satisfaction out of just having completed
the book. I'll let you know if I still think
it's good after my final reading this
summer.

Well, you said you wanted an in-depth,
philosophical letter and I was going to
analyze you and give you my opinion of why

you treat males the way you do. But I've been thinking about another topic a lot lately and I realized today that you fit into that topic, too. So, I thought I'd write on it, for as Anne Morrow Lindbergh said:

"Writing is thinking. It is more than life for it is being aware of life."

A little aside here—that's why I write. It has little to do with publication and money, and nothing to do with fame. I think you would find that hard to understand.

I assumed this was John's grand rationalization, his playing the part of the noble artist who cares nothing for the rewards of art. Now I think he really meant it. He was Emily Dickinson never leaving her room. But just because there was nothing out there he needed doesn't mean the world didn't need something from him. Just because he thought it was silly to want to be known by a lot of unknown people doesn't mean they didn't need to know him. Maybe a publisher would end up crashing into his car

Just because he thought it was silly to want to be known by a lot of unknown people doesn't mean they didn't need to know him.

one day. Or maybe twenty years would pass and a student would find a box of his letters in her closet.

Sometimes in lieu of sending excerpts from the novel, he simply sent progress reports on the character based on me to let me know how I was faring.

> In my book (God! That sounds corny!) your character treats the narrator like he's a little dense but lovable.

I never thought John was dense. Or lovable.

> Your character is very Catholic and won't consummate her relationship with her boyfriend, but he never lets anyone know. I thought I should keep you posted.

My pristine character ends up in jail at the end of the novel, falsely accused of a crime (she crashes into someone's car; John seemed to like that imagery) but unable to defend herself. Perhaps he was working through some residual anger. Other times he would expound on the process itself, even when I caught him midsentence.

Yes, I know-notebook paper!? But I was busy writing and I hate to break my stride. I think my best on notebook paper.

I suppose a good novel doesn't really have one specific theme. If it's good, it has a general area of theme that it concentrates on and then diverges from that into lots of smaller, startling statements. It's interesting but while I write, I of course think and figure out a lot. More and more things fall into place. That's why you and I got along. You see, we are both consciously trying to get things to fall into place.

See, even writing to you has helped me work on the book-has helped me think. That's good-I think I'll get back to work.

He had already been at work. That's what he didn't know at the time.

Poet or Madman

When I overturned the box of my college things at my son's request, the paper about John I had written for Dr. Reed was not the only find. There was a Freud baseball cap in there among the papers—yes, they really make them—but I couldn't find the portrait I had drawn of him. (I need to stop burning things.) There was a journal of my internship at the mental hospital, which included the story of my first marriage proposal (second, if you count John's), from an inmate. And there was a paper on the Hermann Hesse novel that had changed my life, the thing I was actually looking for. But the book was neither *Steppenwolf* nor *Siddhartha,* Hesse's most popular novels, as I had thought. It was *Demian.* I learned from the paper that *Demian* was on the recommended reading list for the Honors English program at my college, so I read it, along with a slew of other books, the summer before I moved south. I always assumed we read the book in John's class, since he referenced it in our letters. But I had read it on my own. There is not a single plot detail about the book in the paper, but that's not why Dr. Reed gave me a B+ (after all, he had promised A's). He gave me a B+ because my style was too dignified, he said, too stiff and formal; the words needed to let down their guard, loosen their ties a little.

He gave me a B+ because my style was too dignified, he said, too stiff and formal.

The reason I didn't include any

plot elements in the paper is because the specific details of what happened in the book are not what changed my life. What changed my life were two passages, two expressions of the same epiphany that Sinclair experiences as a young college student. This paper was another glimpse into my eighteen-year-old self, this time with no pages missing:

> I had always wanted to write, to make a career of writing, and then leave the world with something I had written. I wanted my name associated with some enduring work for which I would be remembered. I had never questioned this selfish goal until it was pointed out to me by Sinclair in *Demian*, when he said:
>
>> I did not exist to write poems . . . neither I nor anyone else. . . . Each man had only one genuine vocation—to find the way to himself. He might end up as a poet or a madman— ultimately it was of no concern.

At this point in my reading, I actually had to stop in order to arrange my thoughts. As I continued to read, I began to cry at how undoubtedly true Sinclair's words had been. He continued:

> Everything else was only would-be existence, an attempt at evasion, a flight back to the

ideals of the masses, conformity, and fear of one's own inwardness.

I had to look closely at myself now. I enjoyed writing. I enjoyed constructing sentences that were unique. Yet, I would struggle over a sentence for an hour so that the words would be perfectly manipulated the way that I wanted them to be. For what? As an inner expression of myself? No, it was a means by which I received praise from teachers. My words may have said nothing, but they sounded beautiful. My goals, therefore, were an evasion. I could not face what I truly wanted to accomplish in life.

At the end of the paper, tapped out by my old college typewriter, was my own epiphany, and a confession.

I was not willing to make my words as strikingly true as they were beautiful to the ear. I realized that I had to fill my words with meaning and that this must come from within.

I was finding out for myself what John had always known about me, about my writing, when he said that it was "beautifully constructed but little depth," with "all the bullshit phrased beautifully, but not an iota of individuality." I had been writing for an audience, for Mrs. B., for Dr. Reed, even

for John when he was only my teacher. I now had an account, on this shiny and smeared
typing paper, of the exact moment   *Writing has to be strikingly*
I learned what it takes to be a   *true, not just beautiful,*
writer: you first have to know   *and to be true it has to be*
yourself; then you have to express   *covered in dirt and blood.*
that self vulnerably. Writing has
to be strikingly true, not just
beautiful, and to be true it has to be covered in dirt and
blood.

I wish I had held on to this insight, let it sink in. But I
was too antsy. In the paper I write about how disconcerting it
is to try to think deep thoughts, to try to find the way to myself while my friends are obsessing over alcohol and guys: "I
almost wanted to pull myself back into the world of superfici-
ality because it was easier to think about booze and boys than
to look at myself as if I were naked and alone." (The *naked
and alone* part is straight from *Demian,* although it sounds
like something embarrassing my eighteen-year-old self might
say.) Instead, I put my clothes back on and booked the first
flight back to the ideals of the masses. No wonder John was
so frustrated with me; I knew what I needed to do and refused to do it. Refused to do it for many years. But I wasn't
the only one. John knew what it took to be a writer, too—had
learned it from *Demian* and hundreds of other novels he had
read about self-discovery—and I'm convinced he knew himself, had found the way to himself. What he refused to do
was the second part, to express that self vulnerably. You can't

just know; you have to show. You can't be afraid of your own inwardness.

This paper was another piece of the puzzle, another way to construct a picture of my life at that time, without the help of my journals. It was like a scavenger hunt, finding the right clue at the right time. New colors, contours were added to my picture by well-timed, carefully placed discoveries—a paper (well, two-thirds of a paper) with my first impressions of John captured in it, a dream that gave me insight, my eighteen-year-old response to a book that foreshadowed my relationship with John.

The idea of constructing a picture of my life piece by piece is reminiscent of a scene in *Demian*. Sinclair is away at school, dealing with social pressures and a drinking problem (I can hear John say, "Sound familiar?"), when he begins to paint a portrait. He thinks it is of a woman he has seen on the street, a muse he feels sure has called him to live a higher life. But he keeps working at the portrait, and it begins to change shape. The features become less delicate. He paints and paints, layer upon layer, until he has it exactly right. He knows he has ceased to paint the woman, but doesn't know who has taken her place. He awakens from a dream, and suddenly it is clear to him. It is a portrait of his friend Demian, from whom he has been separated a long time. And then Sinclair realizes that some of his own features are in the portrait, too. Something within had propelled him to paint a picture of Demian, but in the end he had painted a picture of himself as well.

They were together on paper.

Unmistakably Him

My memory is imperfect. It used to be near perfect, but now I'm starting to forget things. Having clues fall out of boxes is helpful, but even my rendering of John is ever changing. Sinclair says his painting isn't exactly how he remembered Demian (hence his needing to be told in a dream), but it was Demian nonetheless. That's how I feel about writing a book about John, about us. There is a sense of purpose to it, of fate and design; most writers have aspects of their work (correspondence, diaries, the deeply personal things) sealed for a time after their deaths. The typical waiting period is two or more decades. John never intended a moratorium and yet twenty years after his death, I have the opportunity to unseal his letters—by laying bare the relationship that evoked them. But our relationship, as John reminded me in a dream, is still liquid. It's still in motion. The conclusion is not yet set. The portrait continues to change.

It may not be exactly John as I remember him but it is him nonetheless. It is John as the image comes to me, as I try to remember his features. It's at first a mystery (I'm not sure who he is) and then I awake from a dream and he is before me, recognizable. Yes, this is him. Unmistakably him. And at the same time, unmistakably me.

Yes, this is him.
Unmistakably him.
And at the same time,
unmistakably me.

What It Takes

As time passed our letters became more vulnerable; we were less guarded. We still fought a little.

> You say I don't know the adult Amy, which has some truth. I usually only see the teenage Amy. Moreover, though, I'd argue you don't see the real John, either. I admit he doesn't show himself that often (who does?) but he is there.

I believe he was there. He was ahead of me; he was going the furthest. I had only just discovered the directions—knowing myself as my real vocation—but John was already there.

> Quite frankly, I loathe myself for having stopped writing two years ago. It wasn't because I saw writing as not giving me certain rewards: fame or money. You were right. I could care less about those things, especially now.

He didn't care whether he was published or not. He didn't care whether he was a poet or a madman. Or both.

I quit writing because I was so unhappy I couldn't discipline myself to sit there and do it day after day. That, perhaps, is the core of my self-loathing; I can't discipline myself to go on as I always have.

He didn't think he had the discipline, but he did. He hated himself because he had stopped writing. But he had only stopped writing for an audience. His letters kept coming. Deep, compelling letters that had more merit and greater reach than whatever he was working on (or wished to be working on) at the time.

He didn't think I had the patience, but I do. I have learned to sit still. I know what to do with the right books once I've read them. I can think and not just do. But more important still, I know what it takes to write, and it has nothing to do with insights flowing as fast as rain in the store-closet. It is the same prescription for both of us—to know yourself and share that self vulnerably. But to accomplish those two things, we needed each other. That's how we would become writers.

Together, on paper.

6

THE CLOSET NOVELIST

Taking an Inventory of Love and Loss

*I'm capable of admitting I was wrong; I should have
forced myself to live those early years differently.
But I tried to convince myself that I didn't have to have
that kind of love or, at the very least, I would have it,
but later. Yes, I think I was more that kind of liar.*
—JOHN

Sometimes John and I revisited the possibility that our relationship might actually work in the long run, toyed with the idea of marrying and writing books in some seaside bungalow. But the age difference was too much for him.

*I know I promised to write last weekend,
but what the hell—you forgot my birthday.*

Besides, I'm 30 now, much too old to fool around with a mere child of 18.

I guess with my new maturity, my new age, I can see how our relationship would never work. You'd be forever wanting to do the bars and down sweet mixed drinks; I'd be wanting to snooze on the couch and sip on hot milk. You'd boogie down, and I'd just trip. As your hair gets longer, mine would become grayer. While you'd be wanting to..., I'd be wondering...-yes, old age is a horrible thing. Do you realize when you're 30, I'll be 48? And when you're 50, I'll be 68? I must face up to my 30 years and quit leading you on as I have. I'm old-and I'm an old 30 year old.

It was a good thing he was an English teacher because his math skills were embarrassing. He would have been forty-two when I turned thirty, not forty-eight, but it didn't matter because he wouldn't live to celebrate either birthday. He died before I reached thirty, the milestone I was being chastised for forgetting. I have called him an unlikely prophet who saw into my future, but his second sight grew hazy when its eye was turned on him.

If we couldn't marry each other, it was decided, we could at least help the other find true love with someone else. It was not so much matchmaking as thrashing out together what love was and how to go about finding it (there in our little philosophy corner). It was Marilyn Gardner who wrote, "The gift of the family novelist is to turn the cleaning of a closet into an inventory of love and loss." But the letters weren't just our inventory together; they were a record of the other loves and losses in our lives.

> *If we couldn't marry each other, it was decided, we could at least help the other find true love with someone else.*

I feel I'm in a kind of awkward position here. Your last letter is postmarked the 30th and here it is the 7th. That's 8 days—see how my math is improving!—and I don't know whether to refer to N. as your boyfriend or ex-boyfriend!

How you been, Amy dear. Exams are over and I'm back on schedule so it was time to write you. I assume you've received the postcard and newspaper I

*sent to tide you over. I suppose, then, the
first thing we must deal with is the topic
of love.*

John had a very complicated system of love, even if he
had simplified it for his students' sake as either selfishness or
biological reciprocation. He could be philosophical about it.

*I wonder if most people don't "fall in
love" because they're to a certain degree
dissatisfied with themselves. Perhaps when
you truly "love" yourself (and thus the
degree of self-satisfaction is high—I
satisfy myself a lot), there is less need
to love another. Maybe that's why young
people are more romantically inclined;
older people are usually more satisfied
with themselves or at least more
secure.*

He was encouraging me to go easy on myself, for all the
failed romances, the same failed romances he usually rubbed
my nose in. He said there was no reason I should have any

long-term relationships—apart from the one with him—at this point in my life.

But once I did decide to have a long-term relationship, he had a system about how it should work. First, I would have to be willing to be submissive.

Wow! I heard you scream all the way up here!

The antireligious prophet stumping for traditional religion? This didn't sound like something a child of the sixties would say. But he didn't mean it because I was a woman; he didn't think a real love relationship would work unless one partner chose to be dominant and the other consented to be submissive. "You can't fill in *weaker* and *stronger* there or *worse* and *better*," he clarified. "This has nothing to do with that."

Think of it this way. You're drowning, an apt analogy for love. If you fight the water, you'll probably drown. If you take your own initiative and start swimming, you'll very likely head the wrong way and drown. But if you give in to the water—and remember you're in the midst of the *water: you don't know which way is up—if you give in and submit, no fight and no initiative, you shall float to the top. That's what I mean by a submissive role in a love relationship.*

I understood the idea of surrendering to love (I listened to the radio and watched soaps just like any other college student), but why did only one partner have to do it? What role does the dominant person play? "As for the dominant person," he continued, "I'm not so sure he or she wouldn't have to be a bit unfeeling." Here he quoted Isaac Bashevis Singer: "In love you don't do favors. You have to be an egotist or you destroy yourself and your lover." Then back to him: "The only really nice part I can see in this role is that they'd only want the submissive person and no one else. I guess love has to deal with fidelity in some way."

Then he matched me up with another former student to show me how it would work:

Oh, I know what you're thinking—he's egotistical, a bit immature, horribly selfish. Bull's eye: the perfect dominant figure. If he decided he could be satisfied with you or wanted you, you could lie back and be completely and well supported by him. Obviously, your mind would be untouched, but we're talking about emotions here. The brain's only connection to the heart is a physical one. Of course, you'd have to become egoless in your role, accepting the idea of "who's going to know or care in another hundred years?"

Once my role was decided, the only thing left to decide was his. He said he wasn't certain which role he'd like to play, but he made a case for both. Not intentionally. That's my advantage. I have the whole canon of his letters before me. He was never sure what he had confessed in previous letters. Once he wrote, "Love is wanting to give yourself to someone else so you can pretend you're no longer responsible." Case for submissive. Another time he wrote: "I do probably think, romantic that I am (!), that if I were to have a really good relationship with someone, love or friendship, it would be with someone simple where there would be no questions. That person would just be an extension of me, like an arm or a leg." Case for dominant.

There was another case being made in his argument: someone else besides me knew how to write beautifully phrased B.S. without an iota of truth in it.

Of course John never believed any of this, any more than he believed love was two people using each other to get their needs met. It was bravado, another one of his masks. He was still being a reverse alchemist, turning gold into something worthless.

It's a funny thing about poses, masks. Of course, many of them are necessary, but im a real relationship-or a real attempt at a relationship-people have to take off as many of the masks as possible. They'll never be able to take them all off, of course, but as many as possible. How else can two people really touch?

The truth is, I didn't know much about John's relationships outside of ours. There were a few teachers who were close friends, all female, a pattern since his teenage years. He had an affair with an older woman, he confided to me while I was still in high school, when he was younger. (That's another reason I was surprised by his secret.) He spent a lot of time alone. He was afraid to go to bars. For the first time in our relationship

For the first time in our relationship we were discussing the skeleton in his closet like two grown-ups.

we were discussing the skeleton in his closet like two grown-ups.

Finders of Substitutes

Once when I accused John of looking around for my replacement at my high school (he had dispatched Dr. Reed and was now competing with Dr. Armitage), he countered that while he had not found a replacement for me personally, he had found a replacement for my gender. Due to some problems with female students (who were in love with him), the Pied Piper was swearing off teenage girls for good. He turned his magic pipe elsewhere.

As for some new "more plump-cheeked, highly intellectual, amazingly gifted Amy" to catch my eye-fat chance! Besides the fact that there's only one you, I've sworn off female students... for a while. I have decided, however, to not give up, and have instead entered the world of normal teenage boys. They're absolutely fascinating. Since I've sworn off female students, I've had time to start enjoying male ones. And no stupid comments, please.

Teenage boys have no way of showing each other they like each other. I was amazed because as a teenager, I had no male friends and no trouble at all in showing my affection to my female friends.

There were additional research notes in his letter:

It's a whole new world. Teenage boys travel in packs. They're incredibly sports-oriented, but they're as much in need of "listen" and mental stimulation as any of you. They also tend to hit a lot; I'm becoming quite bruised, but I feel it's a small sacrifice for science-the study must go on. Besides, it's just their way of showing affection. I watched one punch playfully at another and then sort of squeeze him around the neck, and it

*struck me how that was really a hug.
Sometimes I feel sorry for these poor
middle class white boys.*

There was something falsely cheery, coolly disengaging about this letter. John assured me I shouldn't worry; it was a grand social experiment, his entering into this pack of teenage boys. That didn't worry me but this did: the disclosure of the social experiment served as a segue into his telling me about a *particular* teenage boy. I knew this trick, had played it myself. Bringing up a general topic of interest because you really want to gush over someone in particular; your affection can be hidden, disguised as playfulness. That was my first clue. John wasn't playful. My college friends and I used to amuse ourselves with a silly card game that was supposed to determine where you would live, what you would do for a living, and who you would marry. Each of the four kings was assigned the name of a real person. I did this little card trick in front of my current boyfriend, and he was one of the kings, of course, but so was someone who ended up being my future boyfriend. I was gushing in hiding. I was also working out his replacement, right under his nose.

John had said that the only thing that really kept the two of us apart, the only thing that would hinder us from real marriage as opposed to fake engagement, was my lack of physical attraction to him. But of course there was more to it than that. I wasn't a man. And he had found the male me.

(That is, me, post-transformation.) A bright, attractive, popular young man who was not a smitten misfit. John wanted me to know they had just talked about me that day, the day he was writing the letter; the young man had once passed me in the hall while I was still in high school and asked me how to spell something and was surprised the future valedictorian didn't recognize the word. He and John laughed about it. She's not an intellectual, John told him, she's a doer. That was vintage John, needling my deepest insecurities even as he works out my replacement.

In his long treatise on love, the one I didn't believe, John included a list of quotes about the topic from his favorite authors, including himself. One was by author and philosopher Iris Murdoch: "Human beings are essentially finders of substitutes." The line is spoken by one of Murdoch's characters in a novel, a cynical intellectual who conducts a social experiment to prove how easily lovers and friends can be lured into making a switch, into finding replacements for those to whom they have formerly pledged undying love. John had found my substitute.

"I really like him," he ended the letter, "and I don't foresee the same problems with him as with female students." But with all those silly crushes he had been the dominant one, the ringleader, the Pied Piper. Now he was giving in to the water.

Lies, All Lies

Eventually I was able to figure out when John really meant what he said. I became a seer, too, able to see through him.

> Your comment on Keats gave me pause. People who say, "I've fallen in love with Keats" or any other writer always make me nervous. Anyway, I never got much out of Keats, and I prefer my physical relationships quite separate from my spiritual ones.

He was always saying things like that, portraying himself as someone able to get his needs met without risking emotional entanglement: "I was alone and was filled with intense longing for love, a hopeless longing, while to judge by my talk, I should have been a hard-boiled sensualist" (another dead ringer, compliments of *Demian*). That was John; he made himself out to be either a hard-boiled sensualist or a self-satisfied poet, like the un-fettered Emily Dickinson. I, on the other hand, had not

"I prefer my physical relationships quite separate from my spiritual ones."

found love because I was fickle and young and insecure and incapable of loving myself, all the things he was not. I had not found love because I was from a broken home; he had an unshakable foundation. So of course I tried to learn from him, to parrot back his great truths.

I think I was most jarred by what you said at the end of your last letter about Emily Dickinson. You said if she had gotten her lost love, you wondered if her life would have been any better. And earlier, you'd written that "the other half" might just lie within ourselves, and we're "too stupid" to realize it. Wrong, all wrong; lies, all lies.

But these were his lies.

I suppose I think about all this now because the one thing I didn't take care of when I was younger was having a relationship. And I'm a weak enough person in so many ways, to have to have *one to be able to survive. I'm sure that surprises you, but it's not a sudden realization. My poses are done very well, but I've never lied to myself.*

He was, however, very comfortable lying to me.

I know my genius; I know my many weaknesses. I should have long ago done something about trying to form a love relationship. But out of fears not connected to the idea of a relationship, I halfway convinced myself I didn't need it—I was tougher than I really was—and halfway convinced myself that it would come in the future. I wonder now if everyone doesn't have to have someone.

I needed only him at this point in my life (according to him), but he needed more than me. He needed something more than his no-divorce parents, his proverbial strong foundation, could give. He was not Emily Dickinson after all; there was something out there he needed.

Since I've had good parents and a few good friends here and there, I could probably suffer through forever... but I choose not to. And yes, some people can do the Mother Teresa bit and make a cause their love, but that's not for me. I'm either not that noble or not that good at self-hypnosis.

He even needed more than his intellect.

The intellect is a wonderful thing, but when it's all you have, it destroys more than it builds up. Graham Greene wrote that those who couldn't fall into a love were doomed to an obsession. It's the brain's way of diluting the destruction it wreaks.

I knew a little bit about obsession, and mine wasn't limited to Freud. There were hand-drawn portraits of other idols that preceded him, even followed him. I have a box in my closet of Elvis stuff—a dozen or so albums, 45s, movie posters, newspaper clippings from the day he died. But hidden among the memorabilia are my own offerings, the things I laid upon his altar, including my own sketches of the King in every style from baroque to abstract. There's even a composition, written in my perfect Catholic girl script, with a five-step process I designed so that other men could become like Elvis. It's embarrassment in a box. The composition is more like a letter, written *to* someone, and I wonder whom I had in mind. I was (just barely) over Elvis by the time I met John in high school, and he was the anti-Elvis so I'm sure it wasn't written to him. The Elvis portraits were of course replaced by Freud. In later years I would hand-sketch Jesus. John's explanation was that I had never been in love before so I was doomed to an obsession. I think falling in love can sometimes become the obsession if the other person doesn't reciprocate. I didn't have to worry about that; my obsessions were unattainable. Elvis, Freud, Jesus. In many ways it was harmless hero worship; all my peculiarities were safe. But not so when the object of affection sits in your classroom.

I knew a little bit about obsession, and mine wasn't limited to Freud.

The Madness of Love

It's funny that I would use John's own words to define love, and he would reject them as lies. The concept of seeking "the other half" to complete ourselves, the one I mirrored back to him, is of course not original to John's system of love, nor did it spring from Emily Dickinson's poetry. It reaches further back, to Plato.

John and I always called our love platonic, and in the modern sense, it was. But Plato's concept of love was more complex than an intimate relationship without sex: in his system man was originally twice what he is, split in half by a jealous god, forced to spend his life seeking his other half. But once the other half is found, Plato emphasized a love that was more spiritual than physical, chaste but passionate, not a lack of interest in sex but a determination to sublimate that interest and channel it into spiritual pursuits for the higher good. That was love expressed properly, the kind that is rewarded in the afterlife. But love could have an improper expression, too. The madness of love can blur a man's vision, especially when there is a difference in age. The relationship becomes lopsided; the older and wiser person refuses to do what's in the best interest of the younger and more naive. Then love becomes an obsession.

Plato's own search for his other half was not always so spiritually minded: as a young man he had an affair with an older woman; later, he fell in love with a younger man. (As far as the difference in age goes, Plato found himself on both sides of the coin, or drachma.) Perhaps at that point he preferred his physical relationships quite separate from his spiritual ones.

Plato's poetic depiction of love, thrashed out in his own little philosophy corner, shows there is much to be overcome to reach his spiritual ideal. He paints a picture of the dueling nature of love, a child of two very different parents. It's a love split in half, even as it seeks to be made whole. On the one hand, Love is like its mother, living in want, born of deep need, regretting its missed opportunity. But Love is also like its father, a powerful enchanter, a subtle teacher, fearless in seeking what it wants.

And that's what worried me. I didn't want to find out what happens when love born of deep need and missed opportunity reaches for what it shouldn't with all the power of an enchanter and all the subtlety of a teacher.

Love as Anchor

Besides the idea that we spend a lifetime seeking our other halves, the other concept that has survived Plato's ancient writings is the link between love and madness. Echoing Plato, Nietzsche wrote, "There is always some madness in love. But there is also always some reason in madness." Plato's hope was that "right-minded reason" would quell the madness of love, that reason would overcome emotion and obsession and release the younger lover if need be. Maybe that's where John got his idea for the dominant and submissive roles in a love relationship, although I doubt Plato would have ever conceived of a lover as an arm or a leg. John thought there was a connection between love and madness, too, but he determined there was another way to look at it. In his mind, love is not madness; it's what keeps us from madness. "Maybe all mental illness," John wrote, "is caused by the lack of a love relationship."

> I tried to sound as if I could live as a single entity when I was younger because I really was too afraid of what I had to do to get what I needed or wanted. Of course, I wouldn't admit to these fears (justified as they are in my situation) them.

He had admitted to these fears before, when we were arguing about masks. Here they are "justified"; back then he called them "well grounded" and "quite necessary." But he called me dramatic when I suspected there was a "world of turbulence" hidden beneath his mask. "No," he countered, "I have too solid a base for that." All his peculiarities were safe.

> But Amy, I really think I rather believe now that mental health is based on how loved a person feels himself to

be. "Love is the only same and satisfactory answer to the problem of human existence" (Erich Fromm). I'm capable of admitting I was wrong; I should have forced myself to live those early years differently. But I tried to convince myself that I didn't have to have that kind of love or, at the very least, I would have it, but later. Yes, I think I was more that kind of liar. Still, I think all most people really need is someone to love them, and yes, someone to love—but we need all kinds of love and all of them satisfied?

It wasn't really a question as much as a plea. That's what was at stake for John. He needed someone to love so that he would not go mad. Love would anchor his sanity. Or unhinge it, depending on whether the someone loved him back.

Second Sight

The only thing I could see that Butley and I had in common was a quick wit and a penetrating intelligence. Besides that, he was a pathetic little man. I am not. As far as playing games, mine are diversion; his were desperation. And if I had once won over the younger guy, I'd have kept him!

John wrote this just after Christmas my first year in college, after I suggested he read the play. He resented my likening him to the main character, an English professor who pursues his star pupil. Things were so different back then, that first year of letter writing. Life really was a game, a diversion. But now things had changed. For a long time I didn't hear any more about John's experiment or his relationship with this young man. And then one day everything fell apart.

His second sight grew hazy when its eye was turned on him.

His second sight grew hazy when its eye was turned on him. It's not that it's difficult to predict the outcome of a teacher–student relationship. It's always inappropriate, always unrealistic.

I was going to say "always uneven," but that's the problem. I don't think John saw it as uneven. It's what made our relationship inappropriate, too; he treated me as his peer before I was his peer. He was by his own admission a genius with the emotions of a thirteen-year-old girl. (Maybe we weren't discussing love like two grown-ups.) I've often wondered why he kept going back to that reference, to that age. It was because something had happened to him in his early teens, something he had never gotten over. It triggered a lifetime of depression. (He only admitted that later, in a letter that came near the end.) I think that's when things stopped for him. He got stuck there. That's why he acted like a smitten schoolboy. In some ways he was one. He was trying to right a wrong, to redo those years when teenage boys would have nothing to do with him. Or worse, he was trying to redeem those "early years" when he said he should have pursued love, reverse the lie he had told himself.

But you can't go back. You can't redeem years. You can't reverse lies. And you can't fall in love with teenage boys.

John patiently waited out the years until the student graduated. Then he declared his undying love. The love was not returned. The young man's other half was a young woman, not a middle-aged English teacher. John had misunderstood the relationship, misread the signs. The student had an unfeeling, authoritarian father; that might have been why he attached so readily to John. But attaching to John meant going underwater. They suffocated under its weight. In the end John lost the relationship altogether.

There are things about John I don't understand. This is one of them. I don't know how he let this happen. His declaration of love caused deep confusion and pain. He nearly ruined the kid's life. I'm still angry at him. My heart still breaks for him.

Fall and Fall and Fall

In the most recent dream I had about John, I enter a bookstore and find a first-edition copy of *The Catcher in the Rye*. There's an English teacher in *The Catcher in the Rye,* Holden Caulfield's former English teacher, a witty intellectual and one of the few adults Salinger's anti-hero admires. Holden gets kicked out of prep school and while on the lam he goes to see Mr. Antolini in the middle of the night. Mr. Antolini warns Holden, tells him what he envisions Holden's life will be like when he's thirty. He is headed for a fall, a terrible kind of fall. And the fall happens to people, Mr. Antolini explains, who are looking for something their surroundings can't give them. It's a terrible fate; Holden will fall and fall and never know when he hits the bottom.

Mr. Antolini doesn't only stand out in *The Catcher in the Rye* because he is one of the few adults (maybe the only adult) Holden trusts. He doesn't only stand out because he gives great advice or warns Holden what his life will look like at thirty. He's also famous for what happens next.

Holden falls asleep on the couch and wakes up with Mr. Antolini sitting on the floor beside him, with his hand on Holden's head, petting him. He says he is just there, admiring. Holden gets dressed, flees the apartment in the middle of the night. There is still wild debate about Mr. Antolini's intentions. He was being fatherly, some say. He was simply showing his affection, others argue. In the literary world, the jury is still out.

But I think the answer is in how it made Holden feel. He wonders if he overreacted (maybe Mr. A. was *only* patting my head) and then says: "The more I thought about it, though, the more depressed and screwed up about it I got." That's the point: no matter what John's intentions, his admiration caused the same reaction in his former student. That's what I can't get past.

Like Mr. Antolini, John was a great teacher, cared deeply for his students, gave great advice—and made a terrible mistake. He wasn't thinking about what was best for his young ward. It was love improperly expressed. He suffered for it. Suffered terribly. But so did others because of him. He went mad with love trying to keep himself sane with love.

He went mad with love trying to keep himself sane with love.

That's the difference between philosophizing about love and living it. Sometimes you don't float to the top when you give in to the water. Sometimes you drown. And when you fall in love, the kind that chooses madness over reason, it's a terrible kind of fall; you fall and fall and never feel yourself hit bottom.

Mr. A. tells Holden that others have experienced emotional and spiritual turmoil just as he does. And their pain has helped others because they wrote it down. It becomes history. It's becomes poetry.

It becomes an inventory of love and loss.

One and Not the Other

Maybe I'm being too generous. Maybe I'm not being generous enough. That's the problem with processing life through literature. It can be an escape. It allows us to couch things in pretty words, in reasonable explanations. What a lovely metaphor Plato has given us. How caring Mr. Antolini is in his advice to Holden, how thoughtful of him to open his home in the middle of a cold December night. It helps me to think these thoughts. It pulls me away from my Mr. A. For a few minutes I don't have to look at him, explain him. But my Mr. A. is not a made-up character in a rambling account of a seventeen-year-old narrator. He's not a portrait hidden in my closet.

The truth is I might never know what John was thinking or why he did the things he did. Maybe his emotional development had been arrested. Maybe he was stuck. Maybe he knew exactly what he was doing. I want so badly to believe it was one and not the other. I want the jury to still be out. But even Plato knew love was equal parts needy beggar and powerful enchanter. It was the first of three blows to our relationship; each one left less and less to hold on to.

He had lost the male me. Now it was just me. He wondered how long before I was lost, too.

I hadn't wondered idly about why you kept coming back to me, and, no, it isn't insecurity, not really. (Perhaps in some way everything is as much related to insecurity as it is to sex.) It's just that on the final level I don't understand relationships. Oh, I understand them probably more clearly than most, but there's a point where it gets fuzzy.

Well, I really do love you, of course.

I suppose if I were happily ensconced in my own love affair, I wouldn't bother myself with the doubts about you and me. It is easier to believe a lie when you're in the midst of it.

He was right when he said it's easier to believe a lie when you're in the midst of it. But this doesn't only apply to romantic relationships. There are other kinds of love affairs. That's why I turned to Plato and Salinger for explanations. If I could attach myself to their stories, process life through their images, then I could bolster my case for what I wanted to be true. Or maybe I was just making it easier to believe a lie.

7

THE BLUE CLOSET

Dream Sequences and Postmortem Visits

Will he come back again, or is he dead?
—WILLIAM MORRIS, "THE BLUE CLOSET"

Something has changed in our liquid relationship. I don't mean something changed back then, years ago, after the incident with the student. I mean now. After writing about it.

John called our relationship liquid in the same dream he intimated I wasn't ready to tell our story. He was right on both counts: our relationship is ever changing, and I wasn't prepared for the changes that would come once I started writing about it.

I'm telling our story as it unfolded, and I'm learning things as I go along, just as he predicted. I see now the difference between his letters that express desperation (and true emotions) and those that were diversion (emotions for show, like anger). It isn't as simple as timing, the idea that in those early letters we were still getting to know each other and therefore not as transparent. We weren't inching our way up the learning curve to intimacy. It's more comparison than timing: now that I've seen his true emotions, I can recognize the fake ones, like experts who train to spot counterfeit money by studying the real thing. Up until now, I only had the counterfeit. I didn't have the real thing until he was broken.

Of course not all of his emotions were fake; there are sincere emotions even in the early letters. But there were more masks than I imagined. He had said that in a real relationship—or a real attempt at a relationship—people have to take off as many masks as possible. He didn't think people could take them all off, but as many as possible. "How else can two people really touch?"

Now that my eyes have been trained, I wonder if there was a mask I missed. I have always been bothered by his angry letters, the ones I stacked neatly in the spear closet (chapter 4). There is something disingenuous about them. The emotion is for show. It's counterfeit. If he is using his anger as a spear, it is for a different reason than I originally thought. It is less to hurt me than to test me: he is setting himself apart from me, he is setting himself above me. Gone are the cheery reminders of how much he missed me, the admission that he beamed for hours after reading my letters. In their place are harsh rebukes, lack of compassion for my broken family, demeaning physical comparisons: you, my anorexic friend, are the White Whale only luckier. Dr. Jekyll

had receded, Mr. Hyde had emerged, the unfortunate con-
sequence, it turns out, of another failed experiment. (Dr. Jekyll invented a potion to isolate his dark side and soon the
dark side took over, no potion necessary.) I thought John
trusted me enough to express his anger, but when I read
back over the letters now, it's not anger I see. It's a play for
dominance. He is jockeying for position. There is a familiar
refrain in the letters: I am better than you, I am smarter
than you, I've got a surer foundation. He wasn't being angry;
he was being strategic:

I'm better than you—

Of course, you'd have to become egoless in
your role.

I'm smarter than you—

Obviously, your mind would be untouched.

I've got a surer foundation. You, as a child of divorce,
need a promise of fidelity—

The nice part is the dominant person
would only want the submissive person and
no one else.

All through the letters he is being (how did he put it?) a bit unfeeling.

As for the dominant person, I'm not so sure he or she wouldn't have to be a bit unfeeling.

Now our liquid relationship feels like ice. He was testing out his theory on me. He was trying me on for size, not as his other half, but as an extension of himself, like an arm or a leg. It was a game, and he was right, his games were diversion. He wasn't really matching me up with a former student to show me how it would work. He was matching me up with himself:

Oh, I know what you're thinking—I'm egotistical, a bit immature, horribly selfish. Bull's-eye: the perfect dominant figure. If I decided I could be satisfied with you or wanted you, you could lie back and be completely and well supported by me.

I didn't yield; I didn't give in to the water; I rose above the submissive role he thought I was suited for. He showed his hand—let me in on the theory—only after the social experiment failed.

He should stay away from social experiments. (Although I'm sure he felt differently about the role of the drowning submissive when he was the one taking water into his lungs.) It was a mind game, those early days. If I had known it, I would have ended the relationship then and we would have never broken through the games to a real understanding of each other. For that to happen, he had to be broken, too. That's the cost of knowing and being known, the hurtful things, the painful discoveries. I'm glad I didn't know it then. I might have tossed his letters into the fire, nothing but smoke and ashes, along with the rest of the things I was too young, or too impatient, to understand.

That's the cost of knowing and being known.

I know it now. And I'm still tempted to toss his letters into the fire. Tears burn as I read his words, as they were intended, for the first time. His experiment was not a complete failure after all. Not then, not now. That's why my voice changed as I recounted his angry letters, why I wavered between myself then and myself now. I was stumbling, falling into the water. But it wasn't hurt that made me revert to my eighteen-year-old self; it was the strength of his control over me, control that transcended the years, transcended his death. He can still change me when he wants to, I confess under my breath, even as I tap out my little tribute to him, even as I praise him for his impact on my life.

Half a Man

I left my tribute to John sitting on my desk, half finished. I thought twenty years had put enough distance between us, but I needed more time. I found other things to do, reorganized my office, sorted through files. That's when I found the slip of paper, tucked in a file where it didn't belong. On it was recorded a dream I had about John. It's not unusual for me to write down my dreams about John; it is unusual that this dream wasn't with the others—those that had been carefully recorded, dated, and filed together. This one had been exiled, and as I read it I remembered why. In the dream John and I host a party together, and I suggest we wear matching outfits. John concedes, throws on the matching clothes, and then midway through the party he is so miserable he changes into his own clothes. I'm embarrassed by this dream, and that's why I left it out of the file. I was trying to change John, dress him up, make him more like me, or more the way I want him to be.

He changed back into his old clothes. Yes, that's what's happening now. John needs to be John, not what I dream him to be. He tried to tell me that in a letter, in a letter that was true because it was desperate:

Is this the me you want to see? Reality is rarely what we dream it to be, Amy. As far as I'm concerned, you'll probably get half your dream of me.

It is midway through the party when John changes into his real clothes. It is midway through our relationship when he tells me only half of my ideal of him is real. I'm in the middle of telling our story when I spot the counterfeit. But the counterfeit is not just John's manipulations, his pretenses and social experiments; the counterfeit is my trying to reconstruct my ideal of him, stacked neatly in a closet. So I return to my half-finished tribute to half a man. I have tried to eulogize a dead relationship; now I have to take an honest look at what is still alive about it.

You Close Your Eyes

Everything shifted when I began to express my doubts about John, when I admitted I didn't really know what he was thinking or doing in pursuing a love affair with a student. It would have been simpler to leave that story out (excising the shameful and the uncomfortable) or explain it away. John saw this tendency in me, my need to take scissors to the bad PR, to spin the story to protect myself, my parents. And eventually him.

Surely you must see that the world isn't as simple as you tend to make it out to be. You close your eyes and pretend you're over all those walls you can't get over, but you're just fooling yourself because you really are still behind those walls. Sometimes I think it blocks your vision.

Now I'm seeing John in a way I didn't want to, dealing with emotions I didn't know I had. It forced me over the wall. He made a point in his letters to say there was a difference between games played out of desperation and those played for diversion, for fun. If I concede he may have been playing games when he was desperate for love, then I have to consider he was playing games when he saw love as a diversion. That's when I figured it out. I wasn't just his star pupil, his betrothed, his Amy Amazing. I was his lab rat. He tried to form a love relationship with two of his students, for different reasons, through different means. One backfired then, the other twenty years later. He should be glad I kept my eyes closed.

I wasn't just his star pupil, his betrothed, his Amy Amazing. I was his lab rat.

When I was still in high school John told me that he had two married friends from college who decided to raise their son with a slight adjustment. From the time their child was an infant, they said "yes" when they meant "no," and "no" when they meant "yes." They would carry out the experiment until he started kindergarten and then set him loose in a world of rightly assigned yeses and nos. John thought it was a grand idea, a flaunting of convention. I thought it was a cruel thing to do to a child. No one wants to wake up one morning with their world upside down.

Upside down or crumbling beneath. Years ago in a dream I had about John (this one made the file), he was situated in a room at the top of an ancient stone staircase. I slowly walk up the stairs to meet him. I hear a noise behind me and look, and am surprised to see that as I've taken each step, the previous stair has crumbled behind me. (I feel sure it's my fault because it was my decision to walk up this delicate staircase in the first place, even though I am walking gingerly with the softest-soled shoes I own.) There is no way for me to get back down. I have to keep moving forward, toward John. He emerges from a room at the top of the staircase and smiles when he sees what has happened but doesn't offer any help. He's done all he can do in bidding me come; I'm on my own regarding the consequences.

Even when I tried to tread lightly, handle our relationship in the most delicate way possible, the truth came out anyway. I wasn't permitted to preserve an image; it crumbled the further along I went.

The Blue Closet

Since I destroyed all of my college journals, I don't have a single account of my and John's personal visits during those years. Maybe that's why I've written down every dream I've had about him in the last ten years. I call the dreams "visits" partly to make up for the lost accounts of real visits but mostly because that's the impression I have when I wake up, that John has visited me. Writing the dreams down is my way of keeping him from slipping into obscurity.

When John visits me, he is often sarcastic and critical; other times he is sincere and vulnerable. In some dreams he is both. That's one of the most common themes of my dreams about John: he shifts back and forth between tender affection and brutal honesty, just like in real life. When the last mask is about to be pulled off, he grins; I can't tell if it's playful smirk or sinister smile. I don't like not knowing the answer. Still I write them all down.

I'm not the first to conceive of dreams as visitations. Freud saw dreams as visits from the unconscious; Jung saw them as messengers delivering insight, so that recurring visitors demanded special attention. Visits can also be inspirational, resulting in complete works of art (the whole of *The Pilgrim's Progress* is delivered by a dream). Other times it is a nightmare that comes to call: Robert Louis Stevenson's story about Dr. Jekyll and Mr. Hyde came to him in a night vision. Upon awaking, he documented the scenes from the dream and penned the story in a frenzy before the images and emotions faded away. From visitation to novel in ten days.

There are not only dreams within dreams but visits within visits. That's what happens in the poem "The Blue Closet," a work of art inspired by another work of art. The dream poem was written by English artist and writer William Morris in response to a famous Dante Gabriel Rossetti watercolor by the same name. The poem is surreal, hard to explain, like the sequences in a real dream. There are a handful of characters, trapped souls who are only permitted to surface occasionally. They share a watery home, a holding cell, a place in between; they are granted release once a year and when paroled, they visit the Blue Closet. Of course there is lingering despair because they are suspended in time, in a state of limbo. Still, they are grateful for their brief respite in the Blue Closet, to be let out every once in a while to be seen and heard.

I don't know if John was familiar with this poem, but I know he felt this way in life at times. In the letter where he tells me I am wrong about him, that only half of what I know about him is true, he confesses his own despair:

I doubt I'll remain your dream of me.
I know I have to make some decisions; I
can't keep going on in this terminal
intermission.

He uses the word *dream* and not *ideal* because I had a dream about him that I included in my letter. I don't know what the dream was about, but I do know he dismissed it as unrealistic. But what he goes on to describe is the exact state of the souls in the Blue Closet: they are in terminal intermission. They never move forward; they never move back. They are perpetually stuck. There's no way to tell how long they have been in this holding pattern, but by the poem's end, the souls are finally rescued from their stronghold, delivered from oblivion. This is the visit within the visit, the arrival of the rescuer. The Blue Closet has been a guiding image for me as I've told our story, because in some ways I see John trapped in such a place. He died young, no one besides his students experienced what a great teacher he was, his best writings have languished. I didn't want John's life as a teacher and a writer to be obscure anymore. He needs to be seen and heard. I want to help him get unstuck; I want to bring him out of terminal intermission.

> *I didn't want John's life as a teacher and a writer to be obscure anymore. He needs to be seen and heard.*

There's another reason I want to release him from this in-between place, and it has to do with my own failure. I was never able to bring him out of the state of despair he faced in life (in truth, I only made it worse). Perhaps I am better equipped now.

The Visits

My postmortem visits with John have been as important to understanding our relationship as our real time together. Of course most of what happens in my dreams is symbolic, but some dreams add new clues, while others provide closure. (One or two dreams even revealed details of John's life I had only guessed at, details that were later confirmed as true.) The visits put a new spin on an old proverb: when the student is ready, the teacher will appear. The teacher will appear, even when he's dead. The dreams are reminiscent of the mysterious ending of Demian and Sinclair's relationship, the two characters in our literary parallel universe. Both characters are called up to serve in the Great War in different units, in different capacities. Sinclair, the narrator, the character I identify with, is wounded in battle. He feels compelled to journey on through the battlefield, semiconscious, as if being summoned. Through the haze he finds himself in a makeshift infirmary, on a mattress on the floor. He turns his head to the side, and is surprised to find Demian there, in the pallet beside him. Demian tells Sinclair he has to go away for good, even though he knows Sinclair may need him again, as he often has throughout their ten years together. "If you call me then I won't come crudely, on horseback or by train," Demian says. Instead Sinclair must close his eyes and listen. Demian will be there, but not in the same way as before. Sinclair then falls into a deep sleep; perhaps he is already in a deep sleep as Demian says goodbye. It may be that this is not Demian's final goodbye but his first visit. The teacher will appear, even when he's dead.

There is a remarkable symmetry to my dreams about John. They come in pairs, two in a week. They are never more than three months apart. Some of them occur on the same day year after year. There are themes that keep resurfacing: they take place in a classroom or a large house; the event is usually a reunion or a party. He is sometimes married to an older woman. In all but one dream he is younger than the last time I saw him in real life and very healthy. (Medieval philosophers speculated that the inhabitants of heaven are all thirty-three years old, the age of perfection, the age Jesus was when he completed his earthly ministry. Jesus does make a showing in one of my dreams about John, and it is John who puts him there.) There are several dreams in confined spaces—a narrow hallway or the corner of a room—and one time I find a closet for us to talk in, but John isn't comfortable enough to stay there. He would rather give up the secrecy than be confined. There is almost always a male figure who accompanies us. At times he lingers in the background, but more often the three of us walk together, arm in arm, with John in the middle. Then of course there is always a lack of privacy; we search for a quiet place to reconnect but rarely find one.

I find a closet for us to talk in, but John isn't comfortable enough to stay there.

When the problem is not a quiet place, it is one of man-dated distance, like the space separating us as I'm climbing the crumbling staircase. I can never go back down, but I also never quite reach him. One time he is in an attic, busy clean-ing (another common theme) and rearranging things. I climb up the ladder to the attic to talk to him, but I am only per-mitted to come halfway. I can't reach the top. This is not John's stipulation. It is something we both know to be true, have accepted as a ground rule in order for us to talk again (like the brief interval trapped souls can enter the Blue Closet and be seen and heard). I am mid-ladder for the whole of the dream. John is upset with me because he has misunderstood my intention. He thought I had gone to grad-uate school for either English or education because I wanted to be like him or because he had motivated me. Now that he finds out I was really studying psychology, he feels betrayed. I am able to placate him by saying he had indeed impacted my life, but in the end he is unconvinced. His disappointment is that I haven't followed his path, not just his vocation. It was this disappointment, and not which major I chose, that prompted him to say in real life: "This is the worst thing you could have ever done to me."

In the poem "The Blue Closet," there is no way to know if the trapped souls are dead or alive or somewhere in be-tween. The only thing that's certain is that they are stuck. That makes them wonder if their would-be rescuer shares the same fate: *Will he come back again, or is he dead?* In one dream John does come back again, or in truth never leaves in the first place. In the dream I am sitting in an editing booth at a TV studio watching a film of John, a taped interview. He looks like he did the last time I saw him in person, not younger as in the other dreams, but just the same. As the segment progresses, the interviewer makes some comments that center on current events. But they are current events now, not current events then. I don't know how this can be. Maybe I'm not paying close enough attention.

In the next scene, I am walking down the hall of an apartment building or a hotel, some temporary location. Out of my periphery I see someone open the door, perhaps to get a newspaper. It is John! Once he realizes he has been found out, he grabs my arm, pulls me into his room. Then I notice that my mother, almost unrecognizable, is also standing outside the door. "She might as well know, too," he says and calls her in. But I don't want her there. There is already too much for me to absorb without her complicating matters.

I tell him I am at the midpoint of writing our story. He says he hopes it is "helpful" to others. Later, I intend to ask him if he would like to finish writing the book together, now that he is alive. (We would become writers together, on paper.)

He never tells me why he faked his death. In every other dream I know he is already dead; none of them takes place in the past while he is still alive. I never saw him dead so it is easier for me to believe he is really alive. I have no evidence that he really died to begin with, except that his letters stopped coming.

In the last scene of the dream I am with my husband and two children. I wonder how John's return will affect our little family, now that he is back from the dead.

The First Dream

I've kept all my journals post-college (post-bonfire), but I never thought about recording my dreams. I started writing down my dreams about John for one reason only: he was a recurring visitor who demanded special attention. I remember waking from a dream so vivid that I not only jotted it down, I drew pictures in the margins of my journal. It was the first account of our visits.

He was a recurring visitor who demanded special attention.

The overall mood of the characters in Morris's "The Blue Closet" is one of gloom. The trapped souls, temporarily sprung, feel isolated. They lack all hope. Existing only occasionally is no real comfort to them. That's exactly the mood of this dream. I stand in the doorway of a parlor of an old mansion. The room is expansive, with high ceilings. The only furniture I notice is a couch, set off to the side. I see that John is sitting on the couch, and I sit down, too, on the other end. I know not to disturb him. He looks so sad. I glance up at the ceiling, to a grand chandelier. There are no candles or bulbs to give light. It is covered in dust. There is so much dust that it hangs in long, wispy strands from the chandelier and ceiling. I wonder if the mess is why John is so sad. I assure him, "I will clean this up for you. I promise." He doesn't say a word; he doesn't even turn to look at me.

I don't know what else to say to make him feel better. I am so happy to see him but my joy doesn't have a place in this room. I look around the parlor, which is poorly lit, because of the dead chandelier, and notice a fire burning in the hearth. There is a shadowy figure sitting to the left of the hearth in a chair. He doesn't speak, either.

And then the strangest part of all: to the left of the ghost by the hearth is a slideshow being projected on the wall. Somehow I know John has put this display together, cobbled together pictures from his childhood. The presentation is easy to see because there is no light in the room except for the fire. But the pictures are not what I expected. They are all of Jesus, old-fashioned and traditional, artwork from the church John grew up in. It surprises me that he would have gone to the trouble to retrieve those pictures, that he would have wanted them at all. Frame after frame is a scene from the life of Christ, faded and two-dimensional, except for one. The only other slide is a black-and-white photograph—not a painting or depiction but a real photograph—of men suffering from AIDS. They are sad, too. John and I sit in silence, nothing but the click, click, click of the slides as they rotate in an endless loop, until I wake up.

This dream has haunted me for years. It reminds me that

what was true in the dream was true in real life: I sat quietly, speaking only to offer simple solutions, while John suffered in the dark, in terminal intermission.

The Rescue

I didn't understand this dream for many years. I wrote down every detail I could in a frenzy the next morning before the images and emotions faded away. Like the characters who inhabit the Blue Closet, John felt that anything was better than limbo. He considered every option. I was too young, too confused, to help him. I continued to give him trite answers to complicated problems.

> Now, Amy, I'm not mad at you and I certainly didn't intend this letter to hurt you in any way. If I were mad or didn't care so deeply about you, I wouldn't have written all this. One thing my latest bout of misery has helped me with is helping others. But you, you buy any inane, simple solution you're presented with. And none of them really work.

Even in the dream I'm remarkably unhelpful. Did I really think his gloom was caused by a dusty chandelier? And my cleaning the parlor would rejuvenate his spirit? I don't blame John for never looking my way. Thankfully, the characters in the Blue Closet face a better fate, are granted a better-equipped rescuer. When the rescue does take place, it is also a reunion. A man, thought to be dead, comes to the mysterious closet to rescue one woman, and in doing so he sets them all free. The death bells stop ringing. The man and woman embrace, share a kiss. They cross a bridge and enter heaven together. They are dead for good. They can rest in peace.

There is a kiss at the end of Demian's story, too. In the final scene of the book, when they are in the infirmary together, Demian tells Sinclair to close his eyes. He leans over the wounded soldier, kisses him lightly. He leaves a fresh stain of blood, Sinclair says, that never quite goes away.

Both are happy endings: two sets of people reunite, and both seal the reunion with a kiss. But most important, from that moment on they are, in the truest sense, always together. Not all stories end so happily, or so cleanly. Sometimes the mark that is left is not a kiss of love or kinship but the stain of guilt. That's what I'm left with. It is there to remind me that I was useless to John when he needed me most. It's a witness to my failure, just like the ghost sitting by the fire.

Why Bother?

Why would I care about failing a man who failed me? He tricked me; he may have even used me. He performed emotional vivisection, for experimental purposes. No one would blame me if I called it even and moved on.

Except that I can't. John was wrong. Maybe he was wrong on purpose and maybe he was wrong without being fully aware of what he was doing. "Jill cannot see what Jack does not know," wrote psychiatrist R. D. Laing. Maybe I didn't see it then because John didn't know it then. He had already admitted there were aspects of him we'd never covered. But I think there were aspects of him he never knew. Now neither of us will know for certain.

What I do know for certain is that he plucked me out of a classroom of students and gave me the confidence to write. He put me in charge of his newspaper. He taught me how to think, how to form opinions, how to cause trouble with my editorials. He wrote me long letters to help me navigate through the transition from childhood to adulthood. He encouraged me to read great books. He processed life through literature with me. He saw through me. He was the one person I couldn't fool.

He was the one person I couldn't fool.

To release John from the Blue Closet means more than making his life known, or righting a wrong. It's more than abandoning my ideal of him. It means forgiving him if he did know what he was doing, pitying him if he didn't.

John is changing back into his real clothes. But that's not the only dream I had about a change in wardrobe. (Recurring themes also demand special attention.) Once it was my turn. I had flown to see him at his home; in this dream I go to him. I am the visitant. He is healthy and in good spirits despite having just received a troubling diagnosis from his doctor. (In the convoluted way dreams work, he is also pregnant in this dream, a hope of new life despite the death sentence.) I am worried about him, but leave him for a time to roam through the small village where he lives. I am trying to find a place to change my clothes. I am frantically searching through town, from place to place, when I push through the doors of an old museum.

I walk through several rooms, passing the artwork on the wall. Each is carefully placed, perfectly framed. It's quiet, peaceful. But the farther in I go, the more I find myself caught in a maze of locking glass panels and doors. As I escape one, another closes me in. They're like closets, only with clear glass. If I change in these closets, I say to myself, everyone will see me.

I wonder why I ran into a museum. There must have been something there that attracted me. Was it that every artifact is in its own place, is perfectly preserved? Everything in a museum is frozen in time. Nothing changes, because the books are all closed, the stories have all ended. Nothing new can be added to its history. That permanence appeals to me; I like things neatly arranged, clearly identified, marked complete. But not everything fits there. Some things thaw out, continue to change.

I have said that love is an imprecise science, but it's not a science at all. It can't be quantified or manipulated by social experiments. Yet neither can it be preserved under glass like a museum exhibit.

Am I any different from John? He manipulated me then; I'm trying to squeeze him into my rigid spaces now. But he's not neatly divided into closets and categories; he doesn't revolve around a theme. That's why when I found a closet for us to talk in—in one of the many dreams where we can't find a quiet place to reconnect—he doesn't want to stay there. He would rather give up his privacy than be trapped. He wants his own clothes, open spaces, the truth. It's no wonder I am sitting in an editing booth—more cutting away—when I find out he is alive. Now I'm the one guilty of vivisection.

Time to set him free, not only from the Blue Closet— from obscurity as a teacher and a writer—but from all closets. It wasn't enough to rescue his letters from my closet; now he needs to be released from my simple solutions, my tidy explanations.

John is not the only one who has to change into his real clothes. Back in the museum I am running from closet to closet, afraid to change because the walls are glass. But understanding John, understanding our relationship, requires transparency. I not only have to stop dressing him up, I have to stop dressing myself up.

I stand in my glass box. I take off my clothes, and they fall into a heap on the floor. I look at my feet. When I wake up, I realize they were nothing but filthy rags.

8

THE CLOSET OF GOD

Room for One

As a child then I had almost fallen into the well.
When grown up, I nearly fell into the word eternity,
and into quite a number of other words too—
love, hope, country, God. *As each word was*
conquered and left behind, I had the feeling that I had
escaped a danger and made some progress. But no,
I was only changing words and calling it deliverance.
—NIKOS KAZANTZAKIS, *ZORBA THE GREEK*

John had handpicked two quotes for me at the end of my last semester with him in high school. His trademark as a teacher was this gift to his students, carefully selected excerpts from his favorite books that matched their personalities or his impressions of them. He reserved this gesture for his Honors classes; maybe he thought they were the only students who would appreciate the effort. I still have mine, typed from his typewriter, pasted onto the pages of my high school scrapbook. I handpick quotes for each of my college students every semester as well, in honor of John. I tell them about him, about his impact on my life, on the last day of class, and then I hand out their quotes. It's been the only way I have of keeping him from slipping into obscurity.

The first quote he gave me had extolled the joint efforts of God and Freud: "If God in Heaven failed, there was always God in Vienna. As a team, God and Freud were unbeatable." (Of course God in Vienna had already failed me.) The second quote was the above excerpt from *Zorba the Greek*. It comes just after the narrator tells the story about nearly falling into a well as a little boy. He was trying to enter the magical world he suspected dwelled there, having been convinced of its existence by his school primer. But he soon learned, as I have, that processing life through literature can be tricky.

When the little boy grows up, he continues to make the same mistake. But now he falls into words instead of wells—into concepts, philosophies, other myths—still hoping to discover a magic city beneath. He finds more sophisticated ways to cut a childlike path to utopia, each one more fruitless than the last. I didn't understand the quote's significance at the time, but this was John, again the seer, predicting the next four years of my life: I was only changing words and calling it deliverance.

Francis with an *I*

I have said that I didn't have much interest in God in high school (the subject of the first quote John gave me), but that wasn't always the case.

I was in third grade when I asked for a sign and received it. My first act of obedience was to break up with my boyfriend. My nine-year-old version of "it's not you, it's me" was to ask him to guess the reason I was ending the relationship. I gave him two hints: it had to do with what I was going to be when I grew up and what I was going to be had the initials "m.n."

> *I was in third grade when I asked for a sign and received it.*

His first stab was "medical nurse"—such an excellent guess I still remember it four decades later. But that wouldn't explain the reason for the breakup. Nurses could have boyfriends.

But the right answer couldn't. I was going to be a nun, a missionary nun.

I had been sitting on the swing in our side yard when I received my sign. It must have been holy ground for my younger sister, too; later I found a list of sins for her first confession shoved in the hollow bar that ran across the top of the swing set. Each sin was listed separately, with tick marks indicating how many times each offense had been committed. I had ventured out to the swing set for my own spiritual reasons: I was conflicted and needed some clarification. Had God been pricking my young heart to become a nun? If so, would he show me a sign?

Religious signs and symbols were important to me as a child; I needed the evidence of things seen. An altar constructed out of a tissue box sat on the dresser in my bedroom, with a hole cut in the top to slide a crucifix through. I took that same crucifix one Good Friday and buried it deep into the dirt of the backyard. It was symbolic of Jesus's three days of death, and I secretly hoped it would rise to the surface on Easter Sunday (or miraculously reappear in the center of my Kleenex altar). Instead the dog dug it up on Saturday, and it was impossible for me to offer a reasonable explanation for why it was there. If I had been keeping a paper trail like my sister, I would have added another tick next to *lied to my parents.*

I don't remember asking for a particular sign, that day on the swing, but I do remember looking up and seeing a bright flash in an otherwise clear sky. With the quick obedience of Abraham, who upon hearing he was to offer up his only son, Isaac, departed for the heartbreaking task "early the next morning," I got on the phone and dumped Rick H.

My spiritual progress was on track, and the next year I was chosen the holiest in the fourth grade and given the honor of laying a single rose at Mary's feet during May crowning. Setting my sights higher, I auditioned to play Jesus in the Passion play the following year, having not thought through the crucifixion scene. Perhaps as a way to put me in my place I was instead given the part of Judas, his fully clothed betrayer.

That I could play a male apostle but then be refused as an altar boy was an injustice that led to the first falter in my spiritual path. To right the wrong I created a minor scandal by choosing Francis with an *i* as my confirmation name. No girl at our little Catholic school had ever chosen a male name before, or even ventured much beyond the perimeter of Theresa or Mary or Bernadette or Frances. Of course the difference couldn't be detected verbally, when the name was bestowed upon me by the priest on confirmation day, but it was defiance in principle. I knew and my confirmation papers attested it was Francis with an *i*. Not to be outdone, my friend Rosie chose George as her confirmation name, and my humble saint from Assisi was dispatched by a dragon slayer.

By sixth grade a growing disillusionment convinced me that my sign from the heavens was just the sun reflecting off an airplane and that God had not really called me to religious service. It was a decision conveniently made just before my first game of spin-the-bottle, which would have reinstated Rick H. had he not transferred to another school.

Despite a slight revival of religious fervor in seventh grade ("Jesus is my best friend," I wrote in my school journal) and a tearful night of wondering in high school when Zeffirelli's *Jesus of Nazareth* first aired, I made little spiritual progress beyond my altar-building, crucifix-burying days of elementary school.

My first date in college was to Sunday mass, a date that

ended badly when the young man, a Protestant, took communion. "I think you're going to hell for that," I whispered nervously when we returned to the pew. He didn't know any better; it was my idea to go to mass, a suggestion made because I was a freshman and he was an upperclassman and we had just met at a party the night before. His willingness to take me on a church date would test his motives, I thought, but I hadn't banked on his eternal damnation. We went out to lunch and I never saw him again.

I attended a Billy Graham crusade two years later when the famous evangelist visited the campus, but I couldn't understand a word he was saying. His terminology was foreign to me, and it left me confused and feeling a little guilty (that part I was used to).

I would have a second encounter with the language of the converted when I sold books door-to-door in Kansas to earn money for graduate school. It was my luck to knock upon the door of every born-again Christian in the state. If I were Dorothy looking for my way home, I could easily find it, not by clicking together the heels of my ruby slippers but by praying a simple prayer, or following four spiritual laws. Almost everyone thought God had sent this young Catholic girl to them—a missionary nun in reverse, who instead of being sent out to convert the masses to Catholicism was being sent out to be converted by the masses to Protestantism. After I gave my sales pitch, they gave theirs.

One evening while making my book rounds on foot, I noticed a green car creeping slowly beside me. There was one person in the car, a man, its driver. I made several mazelike turns around the neighborhood to put my paranoia to rest, but still he kept pace. Spooked, I sought temporary refuge in the home of one of my customers who lived nearby. The husband and wife pulled me into their living room, filled with people there for a prayer meeting. Without much prodding, I finally gave in to a month's worth of sales pitches, saying the sinner's prayer just after midnight. It was my twenty-second birthday.

The runaway nun inside me had been cornered and caught.

The runaway nun inside me had been cornered and caught.

The runaway spirit inside me, stalked and saved.

The Closet of God

All of John's letters to me were handwritten, except for a handful. He only typed out his third-person letters, the ones he wrote to me as various characters: Butley, the president of Anal Stage Anonymous (that's all I'm going to say about that), and finally my long-winded, heavily robed guardian angel. There was also a letter that wasn't even addressed to me. It was the Butley character writing to Dale Carnegie, whom John felt had brainwashed me with his self-improvement books. (Later as himself, John followed up: "Now, as for your Dale Carnegie hypnotism, has it ever struck you that you've fallen for a lot of bull in your short years?") Sometimes the mix of characters sent greetings to each other in their letters. But the most interesting invention was my guardian angel, whom John dubbed Angelica. That was only the angel's partial name; the rest goes on for eternity (fittingly) and includes a reference to Camus and some sexual joke I still don't fully understand.

In the letter, my guardian angel had written this:

I was speaking to God (May His
Graciousness Never Wilt) just the other
day about you, when he gave me your
resumé. He thinks very highly of you. I
could see that immaculate-conception look
in his eyes. But you will have to learn to
deal with some things before you can
consider yourself as a candidate for
Heaven.

First, you must give up John. For good.
Then you must leave civilization and
journey to the wilderness where you can
purge yourself of all evil. At this point,
one of two things will happen. You'll

```
either become a nun and glory in the

wonders of Heaven and eternal

salvation . . . or you'll blow up like a

balloon out of frustration.

    No communion wafers for you, my dear

young child.
```

His remark about my blowing up like a balloon and the prohibition against communion wafers was his sideways jab at my eating disorder. (Angelica, knowing my gullibility, would later warn me not to take any wooden communion wafers.) I'm not sure about the nun reference; it's possible I told him the story of the swing set, the flash of light, and dumping Rick H. In any case, my guardian angel is clear that in order to be considered a candidate for heaven, I must give up John. For good. But the exact opposite happened.

I became a candidate for heaven, and John gave up on me.

That was the second major blow to our relationship—when, just after college, my runaway spirit was saved. That's what I meant when I awoke from my dream about the glass box and realized the clothes at my feet were filthy rags. Same experience, different image. I had the dream about running through the glass closets at the museum recently, not right after college, but it stands as a symbol of that time in my life. I felt exposed, dirty, but also ready to change. The filthy rags are a literary allusion, from the one book I hadn't yet bothered to read: the Bible. The prophet Isaiah compares man's acts of righteousness, his best attempts to be good and to do good, to filthy rags. That's how I felt. I wasn't able to make myself clean, I wasn't able to shake the thought that my life had been a sham. Whatever I was trying to do to redeem myself—to fix my broken family, my broken life—was futile. I was only changing words and calling it deliverance. I wasn't John's pristine Catholic girl anymore, never had been; she was just a character in his book.

Emerson called the center of the universe "the closet of God," a place where the soul meets God and is enabled to see all the mysteries of the world the way God does. It sounds like such a wondrous place to be, like a magic city. But my closet of God was the glass box, the glass closet in my dream, the place where I was first exposed. In it I didn't see all the mysteries of the world the way God does; I only saw inside myself the way God does. I was a whitewashed tomb, beautiful on the outside but filled with dead man's bones on the inside. (Jesus used this metaphor to describe the hypocrites of his day, which meant that I had not only a dancing skeleton in my closet, but rotting bones under my pristine cover.) I had come to the end of Amy Amazing, who had gone down in flames, just as John said I would: "Maybe you'll crash now or maybe you won't crash till after college even, but until you do, you have no way to gauge your own strength." It wasn't just my strength I was questioning. The two most important people in my life suffered nervous breakdowns at the same time, and, unable to help or handle the double trauma, I began to look outside of myself for answers. (I only had simple solutions.) The search ended when I sought refuge from a stalker on my twenty-second birthday. I was living John's quote in reverse: God in Vienna had failed, so I had turned to God in Heaven.

God in Vienna had failed, so I had turned to God in Heaven.

John's reaction to my conversion was swift and painful.

What had I converted to? I was the same Amy, chasing after shallow answers to complex problems. What malnourished, hard-drinking child of divorce with a kite tail of failed relationships trailing her wouldn't say yes to a religion that offered a new start, a clean slate, a place to dispose of rotting bones?

What had I been saved from? As far as John was concerned, I had been saved from ever thinking for myself again.

I'm sorry my last letter upset you, but I ended it by pointing out that though I strongly disagreed, I still loved you, and I even sent a cutesy cartoon to sugar over the disagreement. Was I mistaken to think I was writing to a thinking adult?

John was convinced that I had not escaped a danger and made some progress, but was only falling into new words. I had finally climbed aboard *The Ship of Fools,* the book he picked for me after our first class together, the one that most reminded him of me. Somehow he knew early on in our relationship that I had a ticket in hand, that I would, like the characters in the book, turn my back on a life of disappointment and set sail on a voyage to eternity, in search of a magic city. But salvation is illusory, the author concludes. It was no consolation to John that he had been right about me from the start. He would have none of it, not after all he had invested in me.

Amy, Amy, Amy—where did your mother and I go wrong?

Your mother and I. John and my mother did know each other. They were teachers in the same school district, although she taught the elementary grades. John felt compelled to step in as my missing father figure, bemoaning the fact that his careful nurturing had met with a disastrous end.

My mother was the only other person standing in the hallway of either an apartment building or hotel—it's always hard to know for sure in a dream—when John grabbed my arm and pulled me into his room and I discovered he was still alive. I said she was almost unrecognizable, and there was a time in my life when she was. I didn't want her there with me and John; there was already too much for me to handle without her making matters worse. I got my way in the dream. But you can't shut the door on people in real life. She was, after all, the other most important person in my life.

God as Counterpoint

John and I had discussed God before; the subject of divinity came up once or twice in our little philosophy corner. John had a system for God, just as he did for love, and while God remained a philosophical point, John was happy to enlighten me with the assurance of someone who had already hashed out all of life's great mysteries. At first he positioned himself with the neutrality of an agnostic, ever the skeptic but with the concession that yes, maybe, there is a God.

I don't know what is true and what isn't in most cases—the essential core of agnosticism. It could be there is nothing so I could have lived my life riotously and not worried about the consequences. But, I can't prove that. It could be there is something, and that is the way to live. But, I can't find that. So, since I can *prove neither side, I figure my purpose is to seek a purpose and spend my life on it. So if I die and there was no purpose then my life won't have been wasted because there is no wasted life in that situation. And if there is a purpose, a god, etc., then no one can fault me because at least I spent my life trying to find out. And they say logic is dead.*

I'm not sure if John realized he was borrowing his logic from another, but his argument sounded like a variation on what is called Pascal's Wager. The logic was developed by Blaise Pascal, the great French mathematician, who theorized that belief in God is a better choice than non-belief in God, given the eternal and irreversible consequences of non-belief. (If you do believe in God and there is no afterlife, you've lost nothing. If you don't believe in God and there is an afterlife, you've lost everything.) Believing in God then, according to Pascal's logic, is a better "wager," the only reasonable gamble. It was eternal game theory. John was also hedging his bets, and once he covered his bases eternity-wise, he moved on to free will.

Now for christians, free will should be pretty easy to accept. God gave it to us. How does the girl who proved his existence in one paper disprove his gift of free will in another?

I only proved his existence because it was an assignment in my philosophy class, and since I was reading Milton's *Paradise Lost* in English class, I mainly borrowed Milton's proof of God. But then I had to turn around and defend determinism for psychology class, so there was no dissonance for me as there seemed to be for him. I was becoming a cold intellectual, just what he always wanted me to be.

What would be the purpose of the Judeo-christian god without free will? How could we be judged except as his products—without free will...I've always thought he should have only given some of us free will, just those of us who would know how to use it...

I love the way he uses the royal *we* in this argument—or, more often, the royal *us*: God gave free will to *us*. How could *we* be judged except as his products? He should have only given some of *us* free will, just those of *us* who know how to use it. It was nice of him to keep me company. (Later there would be no us, just you versus me.) He was assuming my Catholicism had stuck past the age when he had abandoned his childhood faith, which was eighteen. But at that time I was neither believer nor non-believer. I was just trying to make A's in philosophy and psychology.

> Then too, there's fate. Fate seems to destroy all philosophies. There's not too much play determinism has in being hit by a truck. And an argument for God in this case is who determined what environment you'd have acting upon you. That's the benevolent hand of the Almighty!

He could be downright chummy, even accommodating of the Almighty, momentarily forsaking his long-held tradition of refusing to capitalize his name. But his congeniality lasted only as long as God was a topic of discussion, an academic exercise. When I changed, everything in John's system changed, just as it did when he really fell in love.

He wasn't just upset that I had abandoned an intellect-only approach to life (he didn't think I had much of that to start with); my newfound faith also put us on opposite sides of another issue.

My newfound faith also put us on opposite sides of another issue.

> I've lived my life (my adult life) in the minority in many ways. I'm used to being made fun of.

He never told me he was made fun of for being gay, probably by the very people whose beliefs I had just made my own. Maybe that's why he tried so hard to dissuade me.

> I think christianity is one of the more idiotic set of beliefs. Historically speaking, it's one of the easiest to disprove—the great "borrower" religion. And I feel anyone in this world who believes in an all-loving, all-powerful god is an ass. I've seen and felt too much pain to believe in that chimera.

A chimera is a fire-breathing monster from Greek mythology. John, it turns out, had some fire of his own.

John and Amy

I understand why John didn't believe my conversion was sincere. My family didn't believe it, either. "At least she's not on drugs," my father said when he heard the news. Sure, there were signs of sincere devotion as a child, but since then I had been through phase after phase, from Freud's dark recesses to Dale Carnegie's unsustainable cheeriness. If I hadn't fallen into the magic city yet, there was no reason to believe this well was any different. In their minds I had gone from a lapsed Catholic to a born-again Bible thumper. The truth is I did jump in with the same zeal that marked my other phases, looking the part before taking the time to read the script. I made rash decisions. I destroyed all my journals. I wanted to prove I wasn't that person anymore. I tenderly and carefully sketched out the face of Christ onto canvas from an old mass card, complete with weak eyes and flaming heart. I framed it and nailed it to my wall. I was a poster child, with my big Bible and my fish symbols and my thickened mascara. (I didn't really change my makeup, but John would have appreciated that joke.) I admit that I was a caricature at first. But I was sincere, and the change, which came from the inside out, was sincere, too. It was Tolstoy who said that knowing the way home and staggering along it drunkenly doesn't make it any less the right way. I didn't stagger—I was more cartwheeling cheerleader—but it was still the way home.

John wrote about and quoted from a lot of books in the

ten years of his letter writing. But the book he wrote about the most, the one he encouraged me to read again and again, was his favorite, *Franny and Zooey* by J. D. Salinger. This is the same book I bought for him in a dream. The Franny of the title is a twenty-year-old disenchanted college student, an English major, whose disgust with her life and the lives of other conforming students leads her to a spiritual crisis. She puts all her eggs in one basket, a simple prayer coined by a mystic called the Jesus Prayer. The Zooey of the title is her handsome, highly intellectual older brother who rips apart her simple system of belief once she returns home to recover from her crisis.

That's the whole plot of the book. There is a lot of philosophical discussion, arguments against oversimplification, anger and tears as the female character tries to cling to her newfound faith in the presence of her intellectual superior, who has his own reasons for rejecting God.

How could John have known?

Playing with Shoelaces

My first letters to John post-conversion were worthy of the condemnation heaped upon them, although there had been some reversals in his thinking as well. I had changed my mind about God, and John had changed

My first letters to John post-conversion were worthy of the condemnation heaped upon them.

his mind about free will. His new position was that no one should have it, not even his elite group of "just those of us who would know how to use it."

> The questions are so easy. If he's all-powerful, he can do anything; if he's all-loving, he would want to do everything; if he's all-knowing he would have known not to give us free will. A good parent knows when to allow a child to make his own decisions and when not to.

He rejected the idea of God because God had failed to be a good parent (and since he had good parents, this was no idle comparison). Something had changed from the time we had our first conversation about free will until now. Had he exercised his free will and made some decisions he regretted? Maybe his free will had infringed upon the will of another and nearly ruined a young man's life.

His agnosticism also hardened into something with less wiggle room. To hell with Pascal and his wager and his logic. It was getting warmer in our philosophy corner.

> And I find it a little amusing when smug middle class people just can't understand

why others can't believe in god. You have a
messy family, but you also have food,
clothing, shelter. No one's tortured you
lately. The bars are still open. There
are still guys around to lay you because
you're pretty. Is it any wonder you believe
in a god...tell it to a starving Ethiopian.

And he was still being nice.

My first attempts at proselytizing were also met with the
scorn they deserved. No one would be issuing me a white
suit or a portable tent anytime soon. Had I really asked John
to "try God"?

How can I take you seriously when you
write things like-you've tried everything
else; why not try God? Really, Amy, I
honestly do try not to laugh in religious
people's faces, but you're making that
pretty hard not to do.

As for having tried everything else (so
I might as well try a god), well, that isn't
quite true. I haven't tried suicide, drugs,

alcoholism, rape, the Reverend Moon,
withdrawing from society, sadism,
bestiality, hobby groups, switching careers,
murder, masochism, rationalization
(other than religion), Zen, taking up an
instrument, burying myself in my work,
charity work, blacking things out of my
memory, molesting sheep or any one of a
thousand other forms of escape equally
as effective as religion.

He mentioned animals twice, but I was not about to point that out.

If religion has hypnotized you into
accepting your condition, fine. I wouldn't
pull anyone out of any contentment that
isn't hurting others. But I prefer a little
more honesty than "I'm miserable but I
can't wipe this smile off my face."
    I still love and adore you, Amy
Amazing, but you really do have to do

something with your childish belief in religion. If you must keep it, do what I do when playing with shoelaces. Don't let anyone know about it, and only indulge yourself when you're alone.

He wasn't really talking about shoelaces, and I wasn't really talking about the gospel. The real "good news" wouldn't be caught dead with my dime-store psychology and self-help platitudes. Thankfully, I would get another chance to redeem myself with John.

Up in Smoke

I have released John from my closets but I still have a few of my own. There was only room for one in my closet of God, not because I didn't want John there but because meeting God only happens when you're naked and alone. I had tried to look at myself as if I were "naked and alone" in my paper for Dr. Reed, the one I wrote after reading *Demian,* the one in which I discovered that I could know myself and express that self vulnerably in writing. But God's

There was only room for one in my closet of God.

eyes are infinitely more penetrating than mine. It's his gaze that rips off the last mask.

Not all of my closet dreams included John. I am alone in one of them, just as I'm alone in my glass box, packing to return home after a long mission trip. (I did become a missionary for a time in real life, so I wasn't exactly lying to Rick H. when I dumped him.) I am packed up and ready to go to the airport when I make one last clean sweep through the room I've been staying in on the mission base. I open a closet and am surprised to see there are some things I have forgotten to pack. I panic. There's no time left. I'll miss my flight. How could I have overlooked such important things?

I overlooked them because I misunderstood what having a clean slate means. Yes, I sincerely came to faith, but I also saw the dissolution of my past as a bonus gift. I had mixed things up: my sins were wiped away but my past was not wiped out. Writing about my and John's relationship and examining so closely my childhood years, my coming of age, reveals that there is more in my closet than my naive understanding of new life allowed me to see.

John saw through me, and his reaction bore a striking resemblance to Zooey's response to Franny's religious shift. In response to the solace Franny says she has found in a simple prayer, Zooey issues a rebuke, telling her the purpose of religion is "not to set up some little cozy, holier-than-thou trysting place with some sticky, adorable divine personage who'll take you in his arms and relieve you of all your duties and make all your nasty [sentimental sadness] . . . go away and never come back."

That was my expectation, too. I sacrificed all of my journals to my own sticky image of Jesus, believing with my whole heart that he, in gratitude for my funeral pyre of rejected words (those I had conquered and left behind), would sweep me up in his arms, relieve me of responsibility, and make all my sadness go away. It was a magic trick, like burying a crucifix in my backyard on Good Friday and expecting it to reappear in a tissue box on Easter Sunday.

But that's not the way salvation works. It isn't a quick fix. Even if it takes place at a certain point in time (say, a twenty-second birthday), it's a lifelong process. The closet of God is not a cozy trysting place, but a relationship that results in transformation after countless encounters over many years. My bonfire accomplished nothing. Not having a record of myself during those years didn't mean they never happened, that they somehow went away. There are still things to be sorted through. There was alcoholism, divorce, anorexia to deal with then. There is pain, death, betrayal to deal with now. There's more to the process than emancipating skeletons or letting the clutter fall on my head. The closet of God wasn't glass just so I could see my sins. It was glass so I

The closet of God wasn't glass just so I could see my sins. It was glass so I wouldn't overlook my scars.

wouldn't overlook my scars. Forgiveness is the antidote to one, healing to the other.

The things left in my closet had never been healed because they had never been acknowledged. Not in any real sense. I didn't think they mattered anymore, now that I was a new creation. But new creations have old wounds. Even Jesus kept his.

Parallel Paths

John always said he and I were on parallel paths but with slightly different ends in sight.

I was always looking for the magic city in the well, trying to book passage on a voyage to eternity.

John was seeking to fulfill his notion of romantic love, searching for someone to love him so that he would not go mad.

For years he had prodded me into greatness, shamed me into moving forward only to discover that when I at last reached my destination, it was a religion that blocked him from reaching his. No wonder he had said of my conversion, on that starlit night on my new campus, "This is the worst thing you could have ever done to me."

Years before his breakdown, John was writing to me as Angelica, my guardian angel, and offered this prediction:

I will just tell you, my dear young child,

that your John has a terrible future ahead

of him. He will die, and sadly.

That's what I was afraid of. I was unable to help him because I had no inner resources, no spiritual reserve. "I will clean this up for you. I promise," I had assured him when I saw his dusty parlor in a dream, when I thought the mess had been causing his sadness, reassured him even as the pictures of Jesus flickered on the wall. But it was a promise I couldn't keep.

2

YOUR COAT IN MY CLOSET

The Gift I Did Not Choose

Your letter made me cry. I'm sure I was something to
you, but that's more to your credit than mine.

—JOHN

The first blow to our relationship was something John did. The second blow was something I did. The third blow was when John did something that I asked him to do. He took off the last mask, revealed the secret beneath his secret. He opened the door to his own exploding closet.

> I hadn't kept my misery to myself out of
> pride; I just couldn't see anything you
> could do for me. You complained I wore
> masks so I told you the truth. Now you say

I'm a whiner. I have decided to stop being honest. It hadn't accomplished anything for me, and was upsetting the people I loved. And, of course, you didn't like the whining.

God forgive me. Had I really called a man in terminal in-termission a whiner? I had combined the positive-thinking nonsense I was being taught in sales with a Pollyanna under-standing of a Christian's new life and fused it all together into a Molotov cocktail that I lobbed in the direction of a drowning man. I don't know why he continued to reach out to me. Maybe it was reflex, an involuntary response; he was flailing, grasping at whoever was closest.

I had never struggled with deep depression, with feelings of being stuck in limbo, but I had toyed with the idea of sui-cide, in the romantic, angst-filled way teenage girls do. The suicide I had in mind would be more of a fading away. I con-ceived of an elaborate plan where I would fly to Hawaii on my sixteenth birthday and don a white dress and a colorful is-land headdress and lay my newly waiflike body on a raft and simply float away in a moment of complete perfection. (My daughter pointed out that there is a popular song on the radio sung by a young woman who gives instruction should she die young: she wants to be buried in satin on a bed of roses and sunk in a river, wearing white. This makes my scenario a little less embarrassing.) There was also the time I wrote an Elizabethan sonnet for English class, for a teacher John hated, about a young girl's suicide. The reference was veiled, though, and I'm not sure the teacher saw it. She gave my suicide an A.

> While lovers may gaze at this sphere of light
> And poets may seek inspiration's beams,
> I find no romance in the moon tonight
> Nor "silver bows new-bent in heaven's dreams."
> Yet when I behold the pitch of its face
> And how it waxes to become a whole,
> The splendor it holds in such confined space
> Very well may unbind my shackled soul.
> But beauty is merely an interlude
> So that time brings me to an end most dear.
> The moon fades now and in my dire mood
> So must I wane with this ill-boding sphere.
> Yet it draws near to haunt me just the same,
> Over the gray stone, tracing out my name.

The speaker of my sonnet (which I titled "Moon Gazing") waxes and wanes with the moon, and then in a fit of despair kills herself. But she and the moon are still connected when, fingerlike, a moon beam traces the etching of her name on her gravestone. Of course I didn't kill myself according to the phases of the moon or die floating on the Pacific Ocean. In truth, starving myself was a much more effective (if less poetic) way to die if that's what I was really after. I usually fasted for a week at a time, but there were two spells that lasted three weeks or longer. I did manage to drink a Carnation Instant Breakfast for final exams, though. My hair was falling out, but I wasn't about to let my grades slip. Anorexia is a death wish, a slow suicide, proving you exist by wasting away. But that was all below the surface, and I rarely visited there.

Anorexia is a death wish, a slow suicide, proving you exist by wasting away.

Your Coat in My Closet

Life is not what we dream it to be, Ms. Sexton.

First I was Danny Saunders in *The Chosen,* then the student lover in *Butley.* Next I was Sinclair in *Demian,* after that Franny in *Franny and Zooey.* Now John was comparing me to Ms. Sexton—the poet Anne Sexton.

Anne Sexton knew despair the way John did. Her brooding poet wasn't for show, either. Shaken by her mother's death (John's mother's death had a similar impact on him), Sexton writes a poem about her, on the day her mother's will arrives in the mail, which happens to be Good Friday. The timing of the will is significant for Sexton, who would not embrace her mother's faith. One of the bequeathals—her mother's fur coat, "your coat in my closet"—settles on her, the poet says, like a debt; it was a gift she did not choose. She describes how her mother's masks fell from her skull during the illness that preceded her death. And then, at the end of the poem, Sexton's mother, whom the poet now elevates to a "god-in-her-moon," returns the favor by making her daughter her inheritor, of a coat she didn't want, of a Christ who still waits for a wayward daughter. I wonder if her mother still reached for her from the sky, like my waxing and waning sonnet moon.

I'm keeping my pledge to John to release him from my closets, but I still have my own, and his coat is in one of them. Like Sexton's mother, John gave me a gift I did not choose: it was his hopelessness, the confidence of his despondent thoughts. In many ways I was still a child; I did not want his death in my closet.

I don't know every factor that led up to John's crushing despair, but it grew worse when he confessed his love for his student, now graduated, and it was not reciprocated. His mother had also died. He saw a psychiatrist for six months ("the right thing to do," his friends told him), but it didn't help. I know he had suffered from depression before, had since junior high, but this time was different. There was some anger still.

If this is the way you react to honesty, to disagreement, to an exploration of pain, don't go into psychiatry. You would be awful at it. I have a fear that the lies you live by might make you think that everybody could buy lies and be relieved. But, you're wrong. There are same intelligent people in the world that will not be suckered into christianity, Dale carnegie, unrealistic literature, self-inflicted diseases or book salespeople.

If he were engraving my tombstone, he would have written: Here lies Amy Amazing, suckered into Christianity, Dale Carnegie (and his unrealistic literature), anorexia, and selling books door-to-door. Interesting that my anorexia was a "self-inflicted disease" but his depression was not. He counted himself among the sane intelligent people in the world not easily seduced, but just a few years before he had something very different to say.

I haven't left the 60s outrageously behind; I first have to work on me for a while and stop wasting my psychic energy on every petty person's petty problems. It's a very freeing feeling as you can see. And another whole, big part of it is attitude. You talked about that that night on the phone. It was something I'd thought about before and hearing you say it (hearing it again), I knew you were right. People can wallow down in the depths for as long as they want, a lifetime. But you can surmount anything. ("Scorn surmounts anything."-camus) When I feel myself getting tired, etc., I simply make myself more determined.

I was talking to that ex-student who has been in and out of mental institutions since she graduated the year before you. And I thought to myself, all she has to do is seize the day, as Saul Bellow wrote, first seize the day.

It sounds like such a simple solution. But that flying optimism soon dissolved into anger, and the anger soon dissolved into despair. It was then followed by humility, vulnerability, even devotion. That was more difficult for me to handle than the despair.

I had seen depression before in my lifetime, in my father, when he gave up drinking. After my mom left him, he would sleep a lot, crawl into bed at uneven times, drown his sorrows in slumber (the benefit, no hangover). My mom was the opposite, always effervescent, always on the move, always tap-dancing. She never missed a beat. Not during the divorce. Not when her father died. And then one day she did. She got sick, threw up a little, lost her mind. Years before, she had gone to the doctor with some hard-to-decipher symptoms. Unable to account for her aches and pains, the doctor asked her a few questions. "What kind of housekeeper are you?" She answered honestly, that she wasn't the best but the house was generally straightened up. "What about your closet?" My closet? "Yes, what about your closet?" It's a mess, my mom laughed, but no one sees that. "That's your problem," said the doctor. "You look great on the outside, but inside you're a mess."

The truth is my mother did not just leave my father. She left me. She left me and my two younger sisters, the only three still living at home. That exacerbated the problems I already had. Some theories about anorexia suggest that the eating disorder is caused by a daughter's over-identification with her mother, an unhealthy attachment that begins early in life and extends throughout childhood. When the daughter reaches adolescence—a time when a child comes into her own as a person, when her personality becomes more distinct—she must separate her identity from her mother's. That's when the natural process of growing up takes an unnatural turn: The daughter's dependence on her mother is unusually strong, and she determines to control herself by controlling her eating as a means of stak-

The truth is my mother did not just leave my father. She left me.

ing out her independence and separateness: I am me and not you. As a bonus, the starvation ensures she will never look like a mature female, more boyish than womanly, and in that way she'll never look like her mother. It stops the process of becoming a woman, and that distinguishes the daughter from her mother even more.

I remember a Saturday afternoon when I was in high school, after my dad had stopped drinking and had been released from the hospital. My mother was upset about something, stormed out of the house, and ran down the hill in the front yard to her car parked on the street. I knew something was terribly wrong (she was crying and she never cried), so I followed her down the hill and screamed after her, "I want to go with you!" She slammed the door, drove off, and soon she had the keys to her new apartment. Later that same day I called her at a friend's house, made some excuse about my sisters to try to get her on the phone, but she wouldn't take my call. Her friend said she was too upset to be bothered.

But five years after that incident, the independent woman who needed no one was clinging to her daughters, cried when we had to leave her, hated to be alone. Once I surprised her with a short visit (I was living out of state), and when I left, she stood at the window as I drove away, nose pressed against the glass, like a ghost behind the curtains. Maybe she whispered, "I want to go with you."

When the psychological separation I was trying to work out as a teenager became a physical separation because of something my mother was trying to work out, the symptoms of my eating disorder intensified. I needed more control over uncontrollable circumstances. That's what I meant when I said I saw the consequences of my dad's secret no longer being secret and graciously declined. You admit your secret, and your mom walks out.

There were other, lesser problems, too. My mother took all of the furniture out of our living room for her new apartment, and we had to make up stories about why the room, the first you enter when you walk in the house, was empty. One of my sisters told a friend all the furniture was sent out to be cleaned. For a year. But despite the lies, the empty room offered irrefutable evidence: our mother has left us. A high school date picked me up at the house one night, and made a big deal out of the hollow room. By the end of the evening, I had dumped him. I even destroyed a photo of the two of us

While my mom was losing her mind, John was trying to convince me he had not lost his.

taken at John's house. Now I have to piece together the interior of John's house from memory. That's the problem with burning the past: you lose the good along with the bad.

While my mom was losing her mind, John was trying to convince me he had not lost his.

I still have my mental faculties. I cannot trick myself into being happy, nor will I. I have had periods of what I call "flying," where though I was still unhappy, I pushed myself to work and act to my fullest. They were great times. The last one ended with my mother's illness and death. But even during my flying periods I acknowledged I was unhappy. To me, being honest with yourself is more important than contentment, especially false contentment. There are problems out there, Amy, that do cause misery. Sometimes you have to hit a certain age before you get defeated by them but others, like hunger and physical pain, can affect *anyone at any age and you won't be able to sing your way through it.*

Or in my mother's case, tap-dance. My mom had tap-danced through the most difficult times of her life, masking her emotions, just as she trained us to do. It was time to pay the piper.

But I had just learned something I had never known about John. He had been paying the piper all along. He had revealed the secret beneath his secret: he was unhappy even when he was happy, miserable even when he was content. There was no evidence that during our spirited exchanges— the up letters, when we competed to see who could do more, think deeper—he was masking a deep sadness. And then when there was a trigger—a lost love, a lost mother—the underlying despair would surface, and he would send up a flare, like a graduation gift with a single quote, a single plea: "This is the pit . . . I am in it. I am alone. I am abandoned. There is no one and nothing to help me."

And, of course, it isn't all just because I couldn't get someone I wanted. That was more a final straw than the beginning of the pressure.

And if you're thinking, why not "fly" now,

don't. I refuse. There's no purpose to it.
I'm tired of doing and not receiving
anything for it except getting the next day.
Although, even that's a stupid thing to say.
I am still doing everything—but writing.

He was still doing everything—and writing. Because his letters kept coming.

Pretty Pathetic

My twin towers of support were collapsing around me, and all I could do was drink my way through my senior year of college. I had always been drawn to John's strong sense of self, his dogged self-assuredness; and even when his abuse was heaped upon me, I was sure it was working to make me more like him. My mom was the same way. She was the source of my "fierce independence," as John called it. I wanted to be like her, but fought hard to separate myself from her. John had asked me in high school what my mom did during the day: was she a housewife? I laughed and told him I had never heard *housewife* and *your mom* in the same sentence before. No, she was not a housewife; she was hardly ever *in* the house. She often joked that she was the one responsible for my independence, mostly through neglect. She was busy all the time, tap-dancing, being happy.

A part of your problem, I think, is that you're now seeing me as someone with a weakness. That's not ego; it's simply fact. I have taken a rather unpleasant existence and made a pretty darn good life out of it. I'm content with my values and philosophical thoughts and what I've done with my brain. I think I'm a fair teacher and all in all, a "good" person, as I would define it. You've seen that side of me, the side I show, and you were—what? Impressed? Filled with respect? Motivated?

I really don't know. That's all part of the mystery of the student-teacher relationship so you'll have to fill that part in on your own.

But now I'm someone who looks pretty

pathetic, and what potential suicide doesn't?

My mother considered suicide, too. What was holding her back, she said at the time, was her paralyzing fear that committing suicide would disqualify her for heaven and she would never see her grandson, her only grandchild, again. She never mentioned whether she would miss seeing her daughters.

An Honorable Skull

I'm finally writing you back; there are so many things I feel I need to explain to you. Some may end up sounding like rationalizations, but they're not. I may be deep in a hole and I may have given up, but I put myself there; I chose to do what I'm doing. I'm sorry if it sounds like someone just aching for a fall from grace (hubris), but I can't imagine

*cracking up or falling apart. Giving up
may not be any better, but it's certainly
different. So as I sit here listening to
Tchaikovsky's 5th symphony, I'll try and
explain some of this to you.*

Ever the English teacher, John puts himself in the place
of the protagonist in a Greek tragedy, one who challenges the
gods with his pride (hubris) and experiences a fall from
grace. Oedipus unwittingly kills his father; Icarus flies too
close to the sun. Now it was John's turn to ache. I want to
put myself in his shoes, in his mind-set, so I listen to Tchaikovsky's Fifth Symphony, too, as I write this, as I reread his
letter. If Tchaikovsky's Fifth helped him to explain, then
maybe it will help me to understand.

*Why? I suppose that's the fundamental
point here-not why I've given up but why
explain it to you, especially if I've given
up? I want to explain it to you because I
do still want to die with an "honorable
skull" (from Franny and Zooey). I gave
up, but that only means I gave up on me.
While I'm still here, I'll still do what I*

*see as my work-for others not for me-as
I always have. And, of course, I'll still
work for those I love, as much as I can.*

John is again quoting from *Franny and Zooey,* his most revered book. Zooey tells Franny that he used to worry about death, perhaps because their older brother committed suicide, but he doesn't anymore. As proof, he tells her he is still in love with Yorick's skull, referring to the most famous skeleton, the most famous rotting bones in literature. It is the skull Hamlet holds before him, of his childhood friend, the court jester, and to whom he sighs the words, "Alas, poor Yorick!" Zooey tells Franny he wants an "honorable skull" like Yorick's when he's dead. And that Franny does, too: "If you don't know by this time what kind of skull you want when you're dead, and what you have to do to earn it . . ." To earn an honorable skull you have to be remembered, you have to make such an impact on someone's life that it will stand the test of time. Then that someone will make sure you're never forgotten, just as Hamlet eulogizes Yorick and commemorates his life long after he is dead and gone.

> *To earn an honorable skull you have to be remembered.*

That's what John wanted. To die with an honorable skull, to leave such an impact that someone would feel compelled to make sure he is never forgotten, commemorating his life long after he is dead and gone.

As for "my whole life being a lie," that was obvious exaggeration, which, like sleep, is a big part of desperation. Basically, the majority of my life has been quite real. I intellectually worked out what was not only right but important, and then worked very hard to live that way. My values and philosophies, and attempting to live them are what give me my honorable skull, what give anyone an honorable skull. The lie part is more one of style than substance, less the "worth of the man" than the personality.

I feel everything and haven't half the "strength" I pretend. I'm afraid of almost everything—"all situations are potentially threatening." If you feel disillusioned to know I'm fearful, insecure, and sensitive, then you've missed the point. It's not what you <u>are</u> but <u>how</u> you attempt to deal with it. Screw the

person that says I haven't tried and
haven't done well. My skull is clear; I'm
content with what I've done.

God Is in Your Typewriter

I have said that when I found at last what I was looking for in life, it was in a religion that blocked John from finding what he was looking for. But John never voiced that prohibition as his reason for rejecting God. All he really confessed to me at the time was that he hated God for letting people starve. His pain went deeper than that, though. In the end I don't think he was angry at a God who kept him from finding love. I think he was angry at a God he blamed for making him different. It was God's fault he was an outcast.

I really don't talk about how depressed I
am with most people (though it is getting
easier to see). Perhaps in your psychology
studies you've come to realize that it isn't
all simple problems of being gay or
whatever. It's the problem of dealing with
what you are.

> I am doing what I can to deal with my problems but I don't feel too hopeful. And if I die, it will be through my own failure and I accept full blame.
>
> Though if there are gods at all, they are malicious.

God was no longer just a bad parent for giving free will to people who didn't know how to use it. He was malicious, he intended harm, was mean-spirited. Anne Sexton also struggled with depression, had a similar problem with the God she blamed for making her an outcast. Her desperation led her to accost an old priest one day, begging him to pronounce her Catholic there on the spot and to administer last rites to her. (Last rites are reserved for the dying, and she had no fatal illness, unless you count the depression.) The old priest refused to do either, but told her something that extended her life: God is in your typewriter.

She sought solace in her typewriter, manically writing the draft of her next book in three weeks. But problems continued to plague Sexton, including her inability to separate herself from her long-dead mother. She called the poem she wrote about her mother "Division of Parts"; the title doesn't just refer to the distri-

"I'm going to have to decide whether John can go on, not whether John can go on for others."

bution of her mother's belongings, but to Anne's attempts to distinguish herself as a person apart from her mother.

I'm not trying to upset you or hurt you in any way; I've spent my entire life trying to help people, because I believe that's the right way to live. So I don't want to hurt you in the end. Still, when you come right down to it, you have to deal with just you and no one else. At some point in time, I'm going to have to decide whether John can go on, not whether John can go on for others.

Anne Sexton decided she could not go on for others. One afternoon she poured herself a glass of vodka, walked to her closet, and took out her mom's fur coat, the one she did not choose. She put on the coat, took a drink from her glass, and went to the garage. She got in her car and started the engine. There she sat in her mom's fur coat until the carbon monoxide poisoned her lungs. No more division of parts, she and her mother were one.

The Final Mask

It was early in my college career when I opened the door to my Fibber McGee's closet, to the exploding closet packed with things I had never dealt with. John was my support in that endeavor, but he was unwilling to undertake the task himself. Perhaps he thought my closet was easier to manage, my soul a little less messy, given my age. At that time he had written:

> That may be one reason why I could never buy the idea of a god—how horrible for anyone to see into my soul. I'm certainly no Dorian Gray, but there are aspects of my life that don't lend themselves to exposition.

Dorian Gray is the main character in an Oscar Wilde novel who sells his soul so that he never ages. He throws himself into a life of hedonism and while his physical beauty is preserved, a portrait of him bears the marks of both his debauchery and decay. John was no Dorian Gray, but he wanted me to know he wasn't the person I thought he was, either.

I do appreciate your concern. I appreciate your love. It's love that's kept me from suicide often before. My father keeps me alive now, just by existing. (He knows nothing of my current state.) But there is a point where one's own loneliness and desperation can override-even a father's love.

And believe it or not, I'm not completely the person I seem to be. Maybe I want you to see the real warts so you don't get sucked into some unreal world of belief in strengths. We're all weak; it's just some are too dense to see the dangers and some are good at self-hypnosis.

Just a few years before John had made a case for keeping others from seeing his weaknesses, and mine, too:

Then there are your insecurities to deal with. It isn't what you think. There, you and

I are similar. Like any smart person,
we know our limitations, our faults, our
own lies. But, like any sensitive person,
we don't want others to know these. We'd
rather protect ourselves in insularity
than be threatened by people knowing us
too well, warts and all.

By *insularity* he meant *isolation,* but the original meaning
is derived from the Latin for "island." John Donne famously
wrote, "No man is an island," and he put the insight in the
context of a man's death: because we are all connected, any
man's death takes something away from me. But John and I
had no idle connection; we weren't just attached in the general way humankind is. If John was going to die, he didn't
want to be drifting alone. He wanted me to see him, know
him well, warts and all. He also wanted me to know he
hadn't lost hope in me.

You're a fantastic person, Amy. I suppose
through all your asiminities I never lost
sight of your potential—I think that's
really why you love me. I always saw you
for what you could be, not what you were;

and I pricked you to try for it. What a compliment, when you think of it. I do still think you're too much on the surface and too worried about Amy, but you'll always be capable of dealing with this if you're ready to.

My response at the time was that if dealing with things below the surface looked like what John was going through—or my mother's vacant stare into nothingness—then thank you very kindly, but I'll pass. No wonder I opted for a religion I hoped would unhitch me from my past. No wonder there were things I overlooked in my closet when in my dream I thought everything was accounted for. Perhaps that was John and my mom's problem, too. They went far too long without opening the door to that closet or, in my mom's case, tending to the mess that no one saw. If you wait too long, then the stuff that falls on your head can overpower you; it can bury you. It might even crush you, to death.

This Far and No More

I know I don't always tell you that I love you, but I do. And I know I'm loved (and "respected") in return. If you don't realize that, it may be my fault of holding back a bit too much. But, if you don't see that love from you as well as family isn't enough, then you don't understand human nature.

John did not buy into the Platonic idea of love as madness; he believed love is what keeps you from madness: "But Amy, I really think I rather believe now that mental health is based on how loved a person feels himself to be." But the love I offered wasn't enough. It was something, but not enough.

> *"Mental health is based on how loved a person feels himself to be."*

Oh, that there were a bit more personal reward in my life. That's sort of the core of my giving up. It's like the Irish way of drinking, marking the bottle "this far

and no more." I've sort of marked my
years of unhappiness that way, this many
and no more.

And, of course, you are special. Don't
get anxious and think I'm saying all
these nice things because I'm suicidal;
that has little to do with it. And believe it
or not, I think you will succeed, through
sheer determination if nothing else.
Never doubt that. But for me, none of that
is quite enough, or quite what I need—need
more than want.

Solitary Walks on Saturday Nights

You may or may not believe this, but the
real reason I haven't written you back
is quite simply I don't know what to say. I
spent some time the last year telling
people how miserable I was, even saw a

shrink for 6 months—"the right thing to do"—
but it was, to me, pointless. Perhaps there
are people in this world that no one can
do anything for; perhaps there are people
who won't <u>let</u> anyone do anything.

I hoped this wasn't the case, for him, for my mom. For me.

I don't know really which is true; I just
know that no one has really helped me
beyond the support of love, which is quite a
lot. I do seriously want to be dead, though
I feel I lack whatever it is in a person
that allows him to commit suicide. That
thought makes me even more miserable,
to realize I could live like this for
years.

    And I know, too, I could end all this
and at least live as I have before, not
happy but limiting the depression and
loneliness to solitary walks on Saturday
nights. Part of me says to do that, but

*part of me reminds myself that
hypnotism is hypnotism, no matter the
method.*

It was almost impossible for me to understand how a man who had given me so much and who had so much still to offer felt his life had waned to such a degree that his choices had been narrowed down to one simple either/or: either solitary walks or suicide.

*Oh, I still teach and deal with the people
I come into contact with, but I know I'm
not doing what I could—I'm not writing.
Your letter made me feel even guiltier
about that.*

I must have given him a pep talk about his responsibility to use the gifts he was given, thinking that would jar him, resurrect him like my buried crucifix. But he *was* using his gifts; he was digging deep and offering what he found vulnerably in his letters. That's what it takes to be a writer.

*Aren't human beings strange? Isn't the
world odd? Some are so fortunate; some
so put upon…and I'm not even a starving*

Ethiopian. But as The Eagles sing, "Things
change slowly, if they ever change at all."
In a way, you're a Christian in the way
you look at me. You can believe in an
all-loving, all-powerful god while children
starve to death and you can respect me,
ignoring my faults. I wonder if I'm
writing to tell you not to respect me.

This hurt me most of all. Gone was the brazenness of the
former days, his self-described brash,
quick-witted exterior. This was not a genius with the emotions of a thirteen-year-
old girl. This was a broken man, my fallen
idol, telling me not to respect him anymore.

*"I wonder if I'm
writing to tell you
not to respect me."*

In one of my letters to my grandfather, I told him a story
about a play I directed in sixth grade. The play centered on
the creation of the world, including the creation of man. All
went well until the actor playing God (the part went to a boy;
I never bothered to audition) switched roles with the actor
playing Adam. Eve would have none of it. She didn't like her
new soul mate. From God to Adam, from divinity to man.
Eve protested the switch, preferred that her mortal man had
stayed God. That's just how I felt about John during this

time. I had asked for the last mask to fall from his skull, but I wasn't prepared for the pain and brokenness underneath. I wasn't prepared to lose my dream of him. He said I ignored his faults, but the truth is, I just didn't see them.

> I still see myself in many positive lights—as a teacher, as a helper, as a moral, principled person. But the years of waking up to gray have conquered so much of me. And the fears I've always lived with (do we all have such fears?) have defeated me each time I tried to cut and run. I doubt I'll ever be able to kill myself—good & bad holding me back—but I doubt I'll remain your dream of me.
>
> I really do love you, and I hope our relationship survives your growing up and my growing down.

I have already mentioned the last part of this letter. John clarified that my growing up was in the past tense, his growing down in the present. I was having the same experience with my mother. I was growing up, and she was growing smaller. She was diminished, crushed under the weight of her own unfinished business, unraveled by her own loose ends. Sometimes I would sit and hold her hand as if she were a child (although she wasn't much for physical affection when we were children). We listened to music together. I even pulled out an old copy of *Jesus Christ, Superstar* and played it on the record player. Maybe he could save her. It was more wishful thinking; a pop-opera Jesus was no better than the pencil-sketched Jesus I had burned my journals for.

I knew my relationship with John would survive, I had written, because I couldn't close his book and walk away.

I called him a book because he called himself a book. But not while we were writing letters about great literature or the philosophy of love or the genius of Freud or even the hypocrisy of religion. He called himself a book in the midst of all the darkness.

Your letter made me cry. I'm sure I was *something* to you, but that's more to your credit than mine. Listen now; I'm not usually openly humble! But, inside I really am. I think teaching, my definition, is one of the most important things in a society. But it's really all up

*to the student. A teacher is like a book-
wasted until he's read. The student has to
do that.*

You've done that.

He always signed his letters the same way: John. But at the end of this letter his precise tiny script spelled out his first, middle, and last name. At first I thought he might be signing a suicide note. But then I realized it was more like a legal document; it was as if I were bearing witness to his last will and testament.

In a sense it was a bequeathal, but he wasn't just leaving his coat in my closet, the gift I didn't choose. He was leaving himself as a book, he was placing his honorable skull in my hands.

He was leaving himself as a book, he was placing his honorable skull in my hands.

10

EMERSON'S LAST CLOSET

The Things I Still Don't Know

*Brief, broken, often painful as their actual meetings
had been what with his absences . . . the effect of them
was immeasurable. There was a mystery about it. You
were given a sharp, acute, uncomfortable grain—the
actual meeting; horribly painful as often as not; yet in
absence, in the most unlikely places, it would flower out,
open, shed its scent, let you touch, taste, look about you,
get the whole feel of it and understanding,
after years of lying lost.*
—VIRGINIA WOOLF, *MRS. DALLOWAY*

I was in bed, waylaid by morning sickness, when I got the
call. It wasn't news that John had killed himself. It was
news that he was dying. The call came from my mother.

Several years had passed since the two most important
people in my life suffered breakdowns. My mom, the one I

recognized, resurfaced just before her fiftieth birthday. John, the one I now knew better than ever, resurfaced—only to be stricken—just before his fortieth birthday.

John was hurt when during my sophomore year of college I compared him to a character in the Dickens novel *Nicholas Nickleby.* It was a Mr. Knag, a man of forty, who was tall and thin and had solemn features so that others were convinced he must be "literary." His sister confirmed this impression, saying her brother read every novel that came out, identified with every hero portrayed therein, and then naturally "took to scorning everything, and became a genius." John loved the comparison, except for the physical details: "And I must admit that I was complimented by your telling me you are reminded of me when you read—although the *Nicholas Nickleby* description you included about the man being forty and with sparse hair I assume was a shot." He was only thirty-two at the time; forty and sparse hair seemed a lifetime away.

John had decided to go on for John, and then his not going on was decided for him.

We stayed in touch, though not as often after I got married. There was an occasional letter or Christmas card or change-of-address announcement. He watched me in a television interview, where I talked about my faith, which had stuck, and he sent his tempered comments. He was happy I was happy. He was happy in his own way, too.

You do sound-content; I'm glad. I think I shall like thinking of you as complacently fat and sassy, like some glistening cat that purrs because she knows how to open the milk bottle by herself.

This was John being John, an insult rolled up in a compliment. If I could call him old and bald, he could call me fat and sassy.

I had not really learned to open the milk bottle by myself, though; it had been opened for me.

But he was right about my being happy. Then the phone rang. All my mother knew was that John was very sick and that she had heard it might be a brain tumor. It's the opposite of what happened in my dream: I am the one who is pregnant when he receives his death sentence. I hung up the phone, sat up in bed, and opened the blinds. I reached for some paper and a pen, and began to write.

Emerson's Last Closet

Things had changed for me in the years following college. I wasn't starving myself anymore, and it wasn't just due to the pregnancy. (Most anorexics will put their disease on hold for a baby, but once the baby is born, it's back to starvation.) But I hadn't withheld food for a while. I had consented, after my graduate work in psychology, to some head shrinking myself, although the truth is my newfound faith had more to do with my healing than anything. There was a lesser need to separate myself from my mom; it didn't require the drastic action Anne Sexton took. Now in a good marriage, I was less likely to blame my parents for their bad one. A lot of people fill their gaping wound, their insatiable hunger, with things: alcohol, drugs, sex, etcetera. And while I had my lot of alcohol (that was over, too), I mainly filled my void by withholding, not by adding to. But the root of that was gone, having been dug up like my buried crucifix— not by a Kleenex-box Jesus, but by the real thing, the real Person.

Now in a good marriage, I was less likely to blame my parents for their bad one.

I began to have a greater understanding of why I starved myself, and I didn't need Freud for this epiphany as much as a geneticist. One of the benefits of self-starvation is the feeling of peacefulness it produces. Not only did it lessen the anxiety that food (and potential weight gain) brought on, it decreased the serotonin in my brain, which led to a scientifically verifiable sense of calm. Anorexics are twice as likely as anyone else to overproduce serotonin; too much serotonin can set off feelings of acute anxiety. When I starved myself (thereby starving my serotonin levels), I was calming myself,

I was regaining control, biologically speaking. My genetic predisposition loaded the gun; my breast buds, my dad's alcoholism, my mom's leaving, and my pining for perfection all pulled the trigger. Many alcoholics, it turns out, have low levels of serotonin, so they try to fill up. I had high levels so I withheld. My dad was addicted to alcohol; I was addicted to calm.

No one's to blame, everyone's to blame. Thankfully, I found a new kind of peace that didn't rely on me, that resides outside of myself instead of inside my brain. I have a sense of that peace almost all the time now, without the starvation. When I was running through the museum of glass closets in my dream, I said, "If I change in these closets, everyone will see." Who I was did change in that glass box, and I hoped everyone would see, even John. Even if he pretended not to.

Emerson not only called the center of the universe the closet of God, but also had a name for the center of a man: it is the last closet, the last chamber. The last closet is that part of a person that is never opened, never fully known, certainly not to others, perhaps not even to himself. And while Emerson believed in the existence of this unexplored internal frontier, this final closet, he also left behind enough writings so that others could come close to peering inside his. I think John did, too, in his letters. There are things, though, I still don't know about him.

I still don't know how he responded to my final letter, the one I wrote in bed after my mom's call, which reached him a few short days before he died. I know he didn't read it with his own eyes because I was told he was blind by then. Someone must have sat by his bedside, read it to him, like Milton's daughters reading back their father's writings to the blind poet.

I still don't know the traumatic event that occurred in his early teens, the catalyst of his lifelong depression, because he never would tell me. That secret is sealed in his last closet.

I still don't know how he came out of his suicidal depression, or how my mother did, or how anyone does.

I still don't know if he ever really forgave me for the "asininities."

Then there are the things John and I will never know together, because John didn't know them himself. As R. D. Laing noted, Jill cannot see what Jack does not know. Then Laing adds: if she did she would be glad to tell him. And of course I would.

There are some things I've figured out through poring over all his letters and telling our story. If I could ever reach John (even in my dreams there seems to be a prescribed distance), I would tell him what I've learned.

What I've learned is that the same person who wounds you is sometimes the person who heals you; the person who pulls you underwater may be the one to rescue you. No one is all good or all bad. The literary term for that kind of one-dimensional character is flat; a flat character does nothing outside the carefully drawn lines of that dimension, whether good or bad. He cannot surprise you.

But a round character is complex, good and bad rolled up

into one. He can still surprise you. Relationships can be flat or round, too. And the greatest lesson I learned from John is that the bad in a relationship does not cancel out the good, and the good does not cancel out the bad. You cry over the hurt, you forgive the wrongs, you embrace what's worthy. You give credit where credit is due. You recognize that you are a round character, too, bringing the same mixture of good and bad into the relationship. There is a cost to knowing and being known, and it's this messiness, these mixed feelings, having to relinquish the desire for something to be one way and not the other, one-dimensional, tidy. What's redemptive about my relationship with John, what's redemptive about every relationship, is accepting this one truth—that it all counts, that the good and the bad are part of the alchemy of loving someone, the baser elements break and boil and bleed, but one day there's gold. Then you are able to say, despite everything: I wouldn't be the person I am today if not for you.

My Last Closet

There were things John still didn't know about me as well. In the years that followed my college graduation, he made an attempt to see inside my last closet. He didn't want to know everything, but he was curious about one thing: why him? Or maybe, why him still?

I must admit that any more, I'm surprised each time I hear from you. It's like I've never taken the time to get a handle on the "grown up" Amy. I think what the small surprise is each time I hear from you is the wondering why I do hear from you. I suppose I'm not certain what you want from me now or what you need-from me.

It would seem that you always manage to have some intellectual relationships (that one male friend of yours in college who's at Harvard or something now, for example) so I can't see me as an intellectual necessity.

What about me? Why do you keep in contact at uneven moments? Somehow I feel there's something you want and aren't getting elsewhere. Or maybe you really do have severe doubts inside you about you. Perhaps I'm like playing with *fire; you talk to me because I emphasize those doubts.*

Why did I come back to him at uneven moments? At first I was probably just trying to save his soul, now that my eternal fate had been secured. But when he reacted so violently to my attempts to convert him, why did I keep writing, calling? It had been the same reason all along: he was the one person I couldn't fool.

He was the one person I couldn't fool.

Affecting Eternity

"A teacher affects eternity," wrote Henry Brooks Adams. "He can never tell where his influence stops." John questioned this assertion, about himself, in the last years of our relationship.

I know you probably won't believe this, but I really don't think I have much of an influence on many kids. Actually, I was semi-seriously considering not teaching after next year, and I think that's good evidence for my not seeing myself as very influential. However, I don't think that's really so much an important part of good teaching as a by-product. I've been forced lately, by various circumstances, to think about what makes up good teaching. Part of the final analysis is that a good (high school) teacher can see his students as human beings. There are a great many people who don't think I should form the close relationships that I do with some students and I had to reconsider this too. I decided, as usual, that I was right, but there's still some thought to give there. I find it difficult to remember the age of my students and sometimes to forgive them their trespasses.

Yes, I had been on the receiving end of his forgetting the age of his students. I was fifteen when I met him, when we forged our friendship. I was ill equipped, still a child. That's why he was so hard on me, had trouble forgiving my trespasses. He kept forgetting how young I really was. Maybe he still saw himself as a child.

> I think my staying power with most students is mainly due to the enigma I appear to be. I'm almost certain that if I explained what appears to be a mystery (and I could easily) that most of the ex-students I hear from would fade away.

That enigma had been stripped away, at least for me, by the letters he wrote while he was trying to decide whether or not to take his life. I was glad to see the mystery go. I appreciated the truth, as difficult as it was to hear. I appreciated his letting me see into his last closet. I might not have been helpful, but I did not fade away. I stayed close by.

Last night I had a dream that I was with a group of people at a friend's house. We were playing some kind of parlor game that involved a series of questions. The playing field narrowed until it was only me, and the hostess took me aside—we were standing alone in the kitchen—and began rearranging my clothes, as if suiting me up for the next round.

"Did I win this round because I knew the answers to the questions?" I asked her.

"No." She wasn't looking at me, just fidgeting with my clothes. "It was because he told you the answers to the questions."

And then I realized all the questions had to do with John, and specifically with the time in his life when he wasn't sure he wanted to go on.

"It wasn't that you knew," the hostess continued. "It's that he wanted you to know." She watched my face as I took in this bit of news and then she went back to tending to my clothes. "He must have really trusted you, because no one else knew."

At first I thought she meant by *no one* the others participating in the parlor game, but she seemed to hint at something more. Her eyes swept over me one last time, and, satisfied I was finally in order, she made eye contact for the first time. "All ready. You'll be going the next round alone."

It never occurred to me that I might have been the only person John told, or perhaps the only person he told so fully. We had written letters for years now; he had already laid a foundation of tens of thousands of words, and those were his letters alone. We could never be that transparent face-to-face or even over the phone; the letters offered both protection and freedom, a barrier and a gateway. He was ready to let the mystery go. John had unraveled the riddle of himself to a student and she did not fade away. "How horrible for anyone to see into my soul," he had said, but someone had seen and she did not find it horrible (or horrible enough to leave him). I knew him, really knew him, and yet the sky did not fall, the earth did not open up and swallow him whole. Maybe that was enough for him to choose to go on.

He did go on, for a few years, and then the next round I would go alone. But now at least I had the answer to why I kept coming back to John at uneven moments. It wasn't for me after all. It was for him. I had become the one person he couldn't fool.

> *I had become the one person he couldn't fool.*

Ginger Ale with Jesus

John had said that if there are gods at all, they are malicious. I don't think he meant it. I think he *felt* it, but I don't think he really believed it. (I was always struck by how strong his emotions were toward this God he wasn't sure existed.) Again I am reminded of *Demian:* "I amused with remarks of unprecedented cynicism, often even shocked [those around me]; yet in my inmost heart I was in awe of everything I belittled and lay weeping before my soul, my past, my mother, before God." John protested when he was most vulnerable. But the real proof was in the character he identified with more than any other, the hero therein, Zooey. His literary twin is a scornful genius as well, trying to talk his younger sister into losing her religion.

Zooey admits he is a little jealous of his sister's ability to believe; he once deeply wanted to believe himself. And then he lets something slip in the middle of their heated argument (most of the heat, as with John, came from him, not her): he had an encounter with Jesus himself, when he was a child. He was sitting at the kitchen table, a bright eight-year-old boy, sipping ginger ale and reading a Dickens novel. Suddenly he looks up to see that Jesus is sitting down in the other chair at the table. Jesus asks Zooey for a small glass of ginger ale. That's it; that's the story. Whether they chatted or simply sipped ginger ale in silence, Zooey never says.

From this encounter Zooey is able to explain to his sister Franny that everyone has a calling, whether it is to act or to teach or to write, and if there is just one person out there watching, listening, reading (or sitting at the kitchen table), then that one person is sufficient. He and Franny and their siblings had all been a part of a radio quiz program when they were children, chosen for their collective genius. Their older brother Seymour, the one who later committed suicide, insisted that Zooey shine his shoes before going on the air. Zooey resists; it's radio, for goodness sake, who will see? But Seymour tells him to do it for the Fat Lady. He never explains who the Fat Lady is, but Zooey begins to picture her in his mind, a fat woman sitting on her front porch, sweating in the heat, swatting flies, listening to her radio all day. Maybe she even has cancer. The radio show may be the only escape she has. From that day on, Zooey shines his shoes for each radio show without prompting from Seymour. After telling his sister, whom he calls "buddy," the story, Zooey shares a secret: "But I'll tell you a terrible secret—Are you listening to me?

There isn't anyone out there who isn't Seymour's Fat Lady.
There isn't anyone anywhere that isn't Seymour's Fat Lady.
Don't you know that? Don't you know that secret yet? And
don't you know—listen to me, now—*don't you know who that
Fat Lady really is?* . . . Ah, buddy. Ah, buddy. It's Christ Him-
self. Christ Himself, buddy."

Franny releases a deep sigh. Her spiritual crisis is over,
thanks to Zooey's secret. Suddenly she feels that all the wisdom in the world is now hers. She is to keep her religion, do
what is in her to do, her calling, and then regard anyone who
watches, listens, or reads as Christ himself. It is Zooey, the
doubter, the tearer-downer, who affirms his sister's faith in
the end.

John told me when I was in college that I was finally
ready to read his favorite book: "That reminds me; I think
sometime soon you'll be ready to read Salinger's *Franny and
Zooey,* sometime after the glow [of being on your own] wears
off." But I never picked up a copy until he died. The first
time I read it I thought, *How can this be John's favorite book?*
How can a book with such a striking conclusion—do what
you are called to do and all who receive the benefit of
your calling regard as Christ Himself—be the same book
he called "beautiful and almost mystical," the one he read
over and over again in order to "ingest it, to feel it"? It's so
hopeful.

Perhaps John felt that way about teaching, even when he
had doubts about his own impact, even when he considered
quitting. If teaching was what he was called to do, then if

there is only one person out there who truly benefits (whether it be the Fat Lady or the anorexic girl), that is enough. And if you treat that one person with respect, if you see what she can be instead of what she is (which is a compliment, when you think of it), then it is as if you are looking into the face of Christ. (This is especially the case if the first time you meet her you tell her she looks like Jesus in *Godspell*.) You've seen something in her, something no one else has. Then that one person, the person you shine your shoes for, the person whose asininities you put up with for a decade, that person will make sure you're never forgotten.

The Dusty Parlor

Some dreams about John stay with me, haunt me. The first is the one where we're pushed into the corner of the room at a high school reunion and I ask if he is still tormented. What did I mean? Tormented by his life, his art, his unpublished novels, his secret? The second dream that haunts me is the one where he sits silently, mournfully, in his dusty parlor.

Seven months after I had the dream about the dusty parlor, I began to read *The Pilgrim's Progress* to my son and daughter. I had never read the classic by John Bunyan before, just as I had gone most of my life without reading the Bible. The book is a famous allegory, delivered by a dream to the narrator. The dream-story chronicles the journey of the main character, Christian, an everyman, who travels from this world to the world that is to come. Along his way he enters the home of a spiritual guide, where he sees a picture of Jesus hanging on the wall. The guide then brings Christian into a large parlor that is full of dust, having never been swept clean before. The man calls for someone to sweep up the mess, but the broom only causes the dust to fly about the room in greater abundance, nearly choking Christian. Then the guide calls for a young woman to bring water and sprinkle the room, and the room is suddenly clean.

The guide explains to Christian that the dusty parlor is the condition of every man's heart. Try as he might, he is never able to cleanse it on his own. The sweeper with the broom is the moral law, living a moral, principled life. But even trying to live a good life is unable to bring any lasting change; it only stirs up more dust. The young woman with the water carries a gospel of grace, not of works, not of morality, but one that cleanses the room, the heart, effortlessly. It is the water of life, the water that washes away trespasses, water that can be trusted because it flows from eternity.

This image in John Bunyan's dream gave me insight into my dream, in fact perfectly replicated my dream. That's why I couldn't clean up the dust in John's room. I didn't have the ability; it wasn't my place. I could not take away his despair or heal his heart. Nor could he. Nor could the vestiges of a childhood faith flashing on the wall.

"You're not so much an intellectual as an accomplisher," John often reminded me. But at some point I realized there were some things I could not do on my own. (He had reminded me of that, too.) I was not a glistening cat who had learned to open the milk bottle by myself. But I did know the source of the water, the one represented in John Bunyan's dusty parlor dream. I knew it in a real and abiding way now, having had my own dusty heart cleansed, my cobwebs exposed and washed away. I thought I had shared that water with John before, but it was fetid, poisoned by my own misunderstanding. He was right to reject it. It wasn't living water.

After Years of Lying Lost

In the epigraph that opens this chapter, Virginia Woolf likens the painful intimacy of enduring relationships to a sharp, uncomfortable grain that after years of lying lost finally reveals itself. In the most unlikely places and only after the intimates have been separated a long time, the grain opens up, sheds its scent, allows you to taste and touch it.

Only then do you understand it, see all sides of it, see all sides of the person. That's what this experience has been like for me. My and John's relationship lay lost, shut up in letters that were buried in a closet. But now that we have been separated a long time and the grain has opened up, I am able to "get the whole feel of it and understanding, after years of lying lost."

It wasn't just our relationship that lay lost. Our relationship had been tied to a time in my life that I had abandoned, wished away. If I hadn't rescued his letters from my closet, I might never have been rescued myself, found those parts of myself that needed healing. No part of my life—or anyone's life—should be ripped to shreds or set on fire. Or hidden away in a closet.

Now John and I are both released from my closets. But I don't regret them. I'm grateful to have shared my secret and to have known his, because the skeleton in your closet isn't as scary when someone else knows it's there. I learned that everyone has to open the door to his own exploding closet, the sooner the better. Even the confusion of the spear closet dissipated and left the understanding that games keep two people at a distance, but brokenness binds them together, makes them equals. I realized that a writer is not someone whose insights flow as fast as rain in the store-closet, but someone who sees himself clearly and allows others to see him, too, through the panels of his glass box.

The cleaning of my closet turned up an inventory of love and loss, and with it the awareness that sanity is linked to how loved a person feels. I know that no one should be left in limbo with only occasional visits to the surface, that permanent release from the Blue Closet is what every soul deserves. And that the closet of God doesn't have room for just one, but one at a time; there are things you cannot accomplish for someone else. I understand now that sometimes you are given gifts you didn't choose, whether it is a fur coat or the confidence of someone's darkest moments. That everything I learned from John is a gift, even the sad moments, even the hurtful moments, even the questions left unanswered. I am glad to have spent time in these closets but also to be free of them. Now I know John in an entirely new way.

It made me happy to get reacquainted with the playful John:

P.S. I do have one piece of good news
for you, my dear young child. You felt
in your last letter that your friend John
was in love with you. Happily, this is not
true. I have it on good Authority (May His
Glory Never Dim) that his desires are
simple—books, poetry, music, nature,
writing, letters, teaching, and a little
wine.

——Angelica

[the rest of the name goes on forever]

Not so happy to revisit the rebuker John:

But if it's a balm to your wounds, believe all you want. I won't hang up on you. I won't be offended by your beliefs or by your lack of agreement with mine. I will judge you by them, but what else can a person do?

It was important for me to remember an elated John:

Write soon. You can't imagine what a kick I get out of your letters. (I'll never try and make you jealous with another girl again!) I just beam for hours after. I read them and I tackle my writing with new vigor.

Even more so a reflective John:

I must admit that I can't imagine being (or wanting to be) anyone but me. Even the lives of those people I've met or read about that I admire, etc. don't tempt me to want to give up John. He isn't perfect and there're parts of him I don't care for, but I can't imagine going anywhere without him. I'd be lonely; I'd miss having <u>him</u> to talk to. With all his baggage he's a worthwhile traveling companion.

I was warmed by the sentimental John:

I uncovered a valentine's card that you had given me in high school where you'd quoted a line from one of my haikus, the line about the purposelessness of living a life without dreams. I still believe that. I still have dreams, and I think you do too. We must just have patience with each other if our dreams don't follow the same path.

Then there was the John who could break your heart:

I still love you, Amy. And I miss you. But I fear I might miss you even if I saw you.

This is how he ended his final letter to me, the one written before he got sick. I don't think he meant it, though. I think he was being mean, or clever. He wouldn't miss me even if he saw me. He would know me. He would know me better than anyone.

He wouldn't miss me even if he saw me. He would know me.

The Last Letter

John was sure I had changed so much that he wouldn't recognize the Amy he had grown to love. But I was still there. The mask of religiosity had fallen off (like all the other masks), and in its place was a deep and abiding transformation, one that allowed me to be more myself, not less so.

I tried to communicate this change to John in my final letter. I asked forgiveness for my trespasses (I was no longer a child who needed a free pass), reaffirmed my love for him, told him he was a teacher who would affect my eternity.

He was my guardian angel, teetering on the edge of his own eternity.

John and I had not lived in the same state since I graduated from high school; I stayed in the South, went on to grad school. That's the last place I saw him in person. He came to visit me, spent a few days on campus. We were both adults now, but I still felt nervous about seeing him. He met my friends, my co-workers, my professors. One professor gave him her copy of a book by C. S. Lewis. "Lewis was a great literary talent," John said at the time, "before he started writing religious crap." We hugged goodbye inside the university library, where I worked. It seemed fitting that we were surrounded by books during our final farewell, even though I didn't have any idea it would be the last time I saw him face-to-face. He was healthy, as happy as he could be: "Still, all in all, I'm happy—at least for me, I'm happy. I believe in the Egyptian idea of balance, so much good and so much bad." If I had known how ill he was when my mom called, I might have flown home to see him, despite the pregnancy sickness. But I didn't know. Instead, I wrote him a letter.

He had just turned forty the month before. He wanted to die young, shout yippee on his deathbed. But I don't think he did because the choice had been taken from him. There was one picture flashing on the wall in my dusty parlor dream that stood out from the others. It was a black-and-white photograph of men suffering from AIDS. I always wondered why that photo was there. Now I know.

The other pictures of Jesus flickering on the wall were

vestiges of John's childhood faith. He said he rejected that faith at eighteen. Zooey's childhood encounter with Christ, like the pictures of Jesus from John's childhood, wasn't enough to bridge the gap, to close the deal. ("And Christ still waits," writes Anne Sexton of her own struggle with faith on the day her mother's will arrives.) Zooey refused to accept what in the end he encouraged Franny to. I think that's what happened with John and me, too. He tore down everything I believed in only to affirm it. He loved me, gave me an example of what it was like to know and be known. In some ways he was my first glass box. I wouldn't have had an emotional construct in place for what it felt like to be fully accepted if not for John. "There are all kinds of ways of ministering," he said in one of his last letters, after he had counseled a former student who had lost her brother in a car wreck. He was upset that I was making such a big deal out of being a missionary, when he felt his calling as a teacher was just as important: "You certainly have my best wishes; sorry I have no prayers to give. But I do have great respect for missionaries and other people who quietly go about doing what they believe in. Be careful in China; they may convert you to Buddhism, Amy— you know how malleable you are!"

He said I was a Christian in the way I looked at him, loving him while ignoring his faults, but he could be equally forgiving, patient underneath all the sarcasm. If he hadn't loved me through my foolish-

If he hadn't loved me through my foolishness, I might never have found the meaning I was searching for.

ness, I might never have found the meaning I was searching for. He stuck by me for ten years past high school, against his better judgment—"I really was feeling, 'Amy, oh well, why bother.' But as soon as I heard your voice I knew I would still bother." I'm grateful he bothered; he was right about being a worthwhile traveling companion.

I don't know what happened on the day my letter arrived. John had long given up his home on Utopia Lane, long given up his desire for utopia itself. I didn't know what his new home looked like; I couldn't clearly picture where he was, what the room he was in might be like. I can only picture him on a bed or on a couch, someone at his side. Perhaps it is the shadowy figure by the hearth in my dream. The person reads my letter to John. Does John laugh? Does he cry?

I try my best to offer water. I wonder if his dusty room has gotten the cleansing he so desperately wanted, the cleansing that would have taken away the despair that was always below the surface, even when he was happy. In the dream I had promised to do the cleaning for him (something I now know I couldn't do), but perhaps the words in my letter—the written word, the epistle, the vehicle of our relationship—moved him to see the cleansing was his for the asking.

Was the blind made to see? I only hoped that John would accept what he had encouraged me to, what he had paved the way for me to.

The death knell stops tolling at the end of the poem "The Blue Closet," because limbo can be a form of death and death a form of release. There is a reunion at the end of the poem: a man comes to rescue a woman in the closet, and with this all the limbo-dwellers are set free. No one is in terminal intermission anymore. The man and woman embrace. They cross a bridge and enter heaven together. They are dead. They can rest in peace.

Sometimes when I'm falling asleep at night I revisit John's visits, with slight variations. I finally make it to the top of the ancient stone staircase crumbling behind me, and I join John in the room at the top. Maybe I tell him all I have learned; maybe he already knows. Or I climb into the attic where he is busy rearranging things instead of lingering mid-ladder. Or we're back in that crowded classroom, pressed into the corner by the mob of students, with the female teacher ever watching, and I look him in the eyes and quietly ask: are you still tormented?

Only this time he says no.

EPILOGUE

I am standing in front of my college students on the last day of the semester. I have a stack of papers in my hands, but they are not final exams. Each piece of paper has a student's name and a literary quote, carefully selected for that particular student. Some students get two quotes. The selections are culled from wildly diverse works, from Emily Dickinson to Anne Sexton, from Hermann Hesse to Chaim Potok, from J. D. Salinger to R. D. Laing. They are quotes from God in Vienna and quotes from God in Heaven. It doesn't matter that this is a psychology class and not English or lit or creative writing. All of John's favorite authors are represented, the ones he taught me in class and the ones he wrote about in his letters.

I tell my students why I chose the quotes and how I learned the ritual from my high school English teacher. I tell them how the quotes he picked for me turned out to be prophetic, a guide to the next ten years of my life and beyond. That he was the seer who saw through me. I tell them how the book he chose for me after our first semester together was number one on the *New York Times* bestseller list the day I was born, and that the number-three book on the list the day I was born was a lesser-known work by J. D. Salinger that would end up becoming an important part of our relationship, too. I tell them about his pink shirts and purple ties and pointy-toed boots. I tell them about the ChapStick, his eternally greased lips, and embarrassing me in class. That he admitted to me after my high school graduation that he was twice as hard on me as any other student in his Honors classes; he had to be, he said, in order to get me to dig deeper, to become the best writer I could be. I appreciate his rigor now in a way I couldn't then, and I guess he would appreciate it, too, given how I've chosen to use the skill he so carefully honed. I tell them that he wrote letters to me, some thousands of words long, for ten years after high school. I tell them he always closed his letters the same way, not with "cheers" or "ciao" but with this:

Enjoy,
John

It was his trademark, like giving out quotes to students. Joy seemed to be what he wanted most for those he loved, that they enjoy life, even if that same joy often eluded him. All of his letters were signed that way but one, and at the close of that letter he left out *Enjoy,* instead signing his first, middle, and last name. I tell them he died young and that I never got to properly say goodbye, never got to tell him how much he meant to me, how much he impacted my life. (Mostly because there was no way to know the extent of his influence on me at the time he died. Those things tend to flower out, open, shed their scent only after years of lying lost.) Then I hand out their quotes.

It's a rite, a tribute, my way of paying homage to John. It was the only way I had of keeping him from slipping into obscurity as a teacher, as a writer. It was the only way I had of making up for never really saying goodbye. But that was before I found his letters in my closet. Now I have another way.

For John. Enjoy.

ACKNOWLEDGMENTS

This story begins when I was fifteen, and one of the problems with being fifteen is that you don't think you need anyone's help. That theory has, of course, been disproven many times over the years; but it is never more untrue than when writing a book, which is anything but a solitary effort.

My deepest gratitude to Rick and David, for your generosity in welcoming me into your family and your lives—and especially for allowing me to share John in the way I remember him.

To Betty Woodmancy, for your friendship and support, and for getting this book into the right hands.

Fortunately for me, those hands belonged to Jonathan

Merkh, Becky Nesbitt, and my editor, Philis Boultinghouse, a kindred spirit with an intuitive understanding of what I was trying to accomplish through this book from the beginning. Philis, you predicted that writing this book would be a "treasure of discovery" and you were right; one of those discoveries was how much it benefited from your careful guardianship and expert touch.

To my agent, Sealy Yates, for instinctively knowing this was my next book, and to my beloved Jeana Ledbetter, whose listening ear, impeccable guidance, and three simple questions brought the center of this book into focus.

To my son, Jonathan, and my daughter, Emily, who now as adults have been a sounding board for this project more than any other since I started writing.

And most of all to my husband, Jeff, for your infinite patience in allowing me to work through the most difficult time of my life, my youth—on paper, in front of God and everyone.